Welcome to the Board

Fisher Howe

. . . .

Foreword by Jing Lyman

Welcome to the Board

Your Guide to Effective
Participation

Jossey-Bass Publishers
San Francisco

Substantial discounts on bulk quantities of Jossey-Bass books are available to corporations, professional associations, and other organizations. For details and discount information, contact the special sales department at Jossey-Bass Inc., Publishers. (415) 433–1740; Fax (800) 605–2665.

For sales outside the United States, please contact your local Simon & Schuster International Office.

Drawing on page 19 of Chaper 4 by Eric Teitlebaum; © 1993 The New Yorker Magazine, Inc.

The material on legal aspects of nonprofit organizations in Chapter Three is from G. W. Overton (ed.), *Guidebook for Directors of Nonprofit Corporations* (Chicago: American Bar Association, 1993). Adapted with permission.

The material on fundraising in Chapter 11 is from F. Howe, *The Board Member's Guide to Fund Raising* (San Francisco: Jossey-Bass, 1991). Adapted with permission.

The passage on liability on pp. 80–81 is from J. Butler (ed.), "Board Members and Risk: A Primer on Protection from Liability," *Board Member* (Oct./Nov. 1992). Reprinted with permission.

The Donor Bill of Rights in Resource A is reprinted with permission from the National Society of Fund Raising Executives.

The standards in Resource B are from the Council of Better Business Bureaus, *Standards for Charitable Solicitations* (Arlington, VA: Council of Better Business Bureaus, 1982). Reprinted with permission.

The standards in Resource C are from the National Charities Information Bureau, "NCIB Standards," *Wise Buying Guide* (Dec. 1993).

Library of Congress Cataloging-in-Publication Data

Howe, Fisher, date.
    Welcome to the board : your guide to effective participation
Fisher Howe. — 1st ed.
      p.   cm. — (The Jossey-Bass nonprofit sector series)
    Includes bibliographical references and index.
    ISBN 0–7879–0089–3 (alk. paper)
    1. Nonprofit organizations—Management. 2. Directors of
corporations. I. Title. II. Series.
HD62.6.H694   1995
658.4'22–dc20

94–43252
CIP

HB Printing   10 9 8 7 6 5 4 3   FIRST EDITION

The Jossey-Bass
Nonprofit Sector Series

. . . .

For
Lydia and Everett,
Lea, Campbell, and Susanna

Contents

$\bullet \quad \bullet$

Foreword

· ·

This admirably slim and lucid volume offers to every current or
potential nonprofit board member a clear and concise guide
with which to assess public service opportunities and responsibilities. What makes an effective trustee of a nonprofit organization? Is
it personality—openness, generosity, clarity of thought? Is it experience and skills that the trustee brings to the governance table from
the world of business, academia, social service, or philanthropy? A
clear understanding of the responsibilities of trusteeship and a willingness to engage one's time and effort to live up to the expectations of trusteeship are probably what count most.

This book is a little gem in the myriad of publications now flood-
ing the market about board membership and nonprofit management. It is especially timely given the difficulties that some
nonprofit organizations have experienced recently. While the book
makes no attempt to cover new ground, Howe's depth of experience
and his straightforward style combine to organize complex issues
into very accessible information for you, the board member. What is
perhaps most refreshing is that he manages to make this guide valuable to both young and experienced nonprofit board members up
and down the organizational scale—from the largest international
institution to the smallest community initiative.

I know! I've served all kinds, and after reading this manuscript
I want every public service board member and chief executive with

whom I have associated to read it, absorb it, and have it available for periodic revisiting.

Howe makes clear and careful delineation between the functions and responsibilities of boards and staffs. He underlines the need for partnership: "Good board members are willing to deal with difficulties yet roll with frustrations. They aren't stuck on winning every issue. They are team players." At the same time, "board members are trustees of a public interest; they have a responsibility to make decisions in the interests of the organization as a whole, not as representatives of any sector."

And bless him, he lays invaluable stress on the importance of a sense of humor!

In underscoring the primary purpose of a nonprofit—public service—he also distinguishes effectively the board's role from that of any business: "The organization exists to serve people, not to reap profits." And "usefulness and effectiveness, not profit, are the meaningful considerations."

This book covers crucially important ground. It does this simply, not simplistically. As a nonprofit board member, you will do yourself and your organization a great favor by digesting it thoroughly.

January 1995   Jing Lyman
                                 Chair of the National Coalition for Women's
                                 Enterprise; former chair of the American
                                 Leadership Forum; board member of the
                                 Enterprise Foundation, the Rosenberg
                                 Foundation, and the Foundation Center

Preface

. . . .

Thousands of nonprofit organizations in the United States are looking for competent board members. At the same time, people in all walks of life are volunteering, or wanting to volunteer, in leadership roles in community activities. Both boards and volunteers are asking the same question: what is expected of a good board member?

Uniting for a common cause and helping others are parts of our common heritage. Inside most of us is an urge to make the world a better place. Volunteering on boards helps to satisfy these needs. Yet Richard Chait and his associates show that the subject is not that simple:

> Nearly all . . . volunteers want to be effective board members, yet most are uncertain about how to do so. . . . [T]he vast majority of trustees are not systematically prepared for the role prior to their appointment to a governing board. . . . [N]othing in life to that point quite prepares you for this role. . . .[T]rustees . . . must draw more upon hand-me-down shibboleths than upon a solid body of knowledge about governance and its influence on not-for-profit organizations [Chait, Holland, and Taylor, 1993].

Unfortunately, solid information is not always easy to find. Library shelves are laden with books discussing nonprofit board authorities, responsibilities, structures, and operations. Few address the subject from the point of view of the individual board member, the trustee.

The purpose of this book therefore is to set out both what is expected of you when you join a nonprofit board and what it takes to become a good board member. The book addresses, almost as in a personal letter, those who are considering membership on a nonprofit board and those already on a board who conscientiously want to see how they can be most effective in meeting their responsibilities.

Discussions of qualities and responsibilities of trusteeship run the risk of oversimplification. Some have reduced the qualifications for a nonprofit board to four *ws*—wealth, work, wisdom, and wit. Such a generalization is fine as far as it goes. But organizations differ greatly in character and purpose. Communities in which they operate—national or local—are vastly different. Broad generalizations therefore do not help anyone seeking to understand all that is involved in trusteeship.

On the other hand, there is risk in making these matters more complex than they need be. Offering rigorous, detailed definitions of each quality and skill a good trustee brings to the board, and every fiduciary hazard that might arise, can be unhelpful—as well as boring. This discussion seeks to tread the line between these hazards and embrace the full range of board membership from novice innocence to worldly sophistication.

Do not, however, expect a how-to book. You will not find a detailed catalog of legal or other requirements to guide trustees faced with the more complex problems of accountability or liability. Nor does the book seek to advance new theories and insights on ways of dealing with governance problems.

Instead of offering instructive solutions, the book seeks to suggest to those already on nonprofit boards, or about to join one, a way of looking at trusteeship. It seeks to help boards that are recruit-ing volunteer trustees, or boards struggling to define the role of their members. It may also be of value to executives and staffs who have a responsibility to help their boards be effective.

Background

Governing bodies of nonprofit organizations may be called boards of trustees, governors, directors, overseers, or regents. Religious con-gregations may also have these bodies or they may have synagogue boards, vestries, or elders. Distinctions can be made among the titles, but here the terms "board member" and "trustee" are used throughout and interchangeably.

Nonprofit organizations come in all sizes, shapes, and purposes. Together they constitute what has come to be known as the third or independent sector, after the business and government sectors. Although traditionally the terms "charity" and "charitable organi-zations" have referred to programs helping the poor and the needy, more recently the terms have come to incorporate all activities and organizations whose purpose is public service. In addition to com-munity services, the broad categories of education, health, recre-ation, and research, even scientific activities, are included. Charitable organizations thus are defined as all entities designated under the 501(c)(3) clause of the IRS Code for tax-exempt organi-zations. As such they differ from other nonprofit tax-exempt insti-tutions, such as labor unions and professional associations organized to serve members rather than the general public. They differ too from religious congregations, which are exempt from the code.

Although the particular purpose of an organization may not sig-nificantly affect the nature of duties and responsibilities of a board member, it will have everything to do with engaging a particular board member's interest and with the level of that interest. An orga-nization's purpose can be to serve the general public or to serve the membership. Public service organizations may serve specific populations defined by gender, age, or racial/ethnic group. Or they can target more specific groups such as those suffering from a particular disease, the homeless, or those caring for animals.

Size, too, will be a major factor in determining the nature of a board. Clearly, serving on the board of a large national organization with a budget of several million dollars will be a wholly different experience from serving on the board of a school or "hands-on" local community service.

A board's activities will vary with the nature of its institutional funding. Operating institutions, such as schools, hospitals, museums, research, or community service organizations, rely heavily on program revenues—tuitions, admissions, fees, charges, and various forms of third-party reimbursements—as well as on contributions. These organizations will not be the same as, say, an environmental organization that is wholly funded by grants and donations, or a richly endowed educational institution. Boards of organizations that are heavily supported by government contracts and reimbursements will handle affairs differently from those that rely principally on foundation, corporate, and individual contributions.

Thus, the purpose, size, and individual character of a nonprofit organization will determine the nature of board activity, the way its program activities are carried out, and the appeal of the organization to prospective board members. But these variables will not determine the fundamental trusteeship role and responsibility. What is expected of a good board member will, with only minor variations, turn out to be the same in all cases.

Overview of the Contents

Part One attempts to put board membership in perspective. Chapter One explores the desire in people to volunteer for trusteeship, and the need to encourage them. Chapter Two looks at the personal qualities that a good trustee needs. Chapter Three is an overview of the fundamental legal technicalities that board mem-

bers should be aware of. Chapter Four investigates the common misunderstanding that a nonprofit organization should operate just like
a business.

Part Two covers the specifics of a trustee's responsibilities. Just
what is it that an organization expects of its board members? There
are in fact seven, and really only seven, responsibilities, and they
are the same for all boards.

These seven responsibilities are summarized in Chapter Five and
discussed in detail in succeeding chapters.

1. Attendance (Chapter Six)

2. Approval of the mission; help in planning (Chapter Seven)

3. Selection and evaluation of the executive (Chapter Eight)

4. Assurance of financial responsibility, including budgets,
   audits, and investments (Chapter Nine)

5. Support and oversight of programs (Chapter Ten)

6. Participation in fundraising (Chapter Eleven)

7. Assurance of board effectiveness (Chapter Twelve)

Part Three addresses three other matters, not directly responsibilities, that should concern a trustee. The board's organization and procedures—composition, recruitment of members, officers, committee
structure, and meetings—are all important elements in the overall
effectiveness of the board; these are described in Chapter Thirteen.

Chapter Fourteen looks at the other side of the coin: what a
trustee has the right to expect in return from an organization; it covers the obligations and liabilities that go with trusteeship. Finally,
the question of leadership—what it involves, how it should be
maintained—is discussed in Chapter Fifteen.

People considering service on a nonprofit board, as well as those
already serving, have legitimate questions to ask, and perhaps some
doubts. A selection of such questions follows some of the chapter
texts.

Acknowledgments

Once again I owe an incalculable debt to my brother, David L. Howe of Charlotte, North Carolina, for the endless hours he has devoted to successive drafts of this manuscript and the masterful changes he has wrought in them. I am also indebted for major assistance rendered by my oldest and closest friend, Dr. Francis D. Moore of Boston; quite apart from being a world-class surgeon, he is himself an experienced trustee. But don't blame them for errors or provocative judgments.

Washington, D.C.   Fisher Howe
January 1995

The Author

· ·

Fisher Howe is a consultant for nonprofit organizations with the firm of Lavender/Howe & Associates, which has offices in Ojai, California, and Washington, D.C. He received his B.A. (1935) from Harvard University in history and literature and later had a full career in the Foreign Service. He has served as assistant dean and executive director at the Johns Hopkins University School of Advanced International Studies, and as director of institutional relations for Resources for the Future, a Washington, D.C., research organization for energy, natural resources, and the environment.

Howe has been a trustee of several organizations, including Fountain Valley School in Colorado Springs, Hospice of D.C., Washington Area Council on Alcohol and Drug Abuse, Metropolitan Washington United Way, Institute for Circadian Physiology in Boston, Bureau of Rehabilitation (offender halfway houses), Pilgrim Society (Plymouth, Massachusetts), and the Washington chapter of the National Society of Fund Raising Executives.

His publications include "What You Need to Know About Fund Raising," *Harvard Business Review* (1986); "Fund Raising and the Nonprofit Board Member," National Center for Nonprofit Boards (1988); and *The Board Member's Guide to Fund Raising* (1991).

Welcome to the Board

Part I

· ·

Board Membership in Perspective

1
· ·

On Joining a Board

Our country's nonprofit organizations range from great universities to the smallest of community service agencies. Whether they cover the arts, education, health care, community welfare, recreation, or public policy, and whether they deal with the homeless, with drug and alcohol sufferers, with children or the aged, they have one thing in common: they all need help. They need volunteers skilled in financial management, public relations, fundraising, and strategic planning. They need leadership. They need lively, dedicated volunteer board members.

As a board member or prospective board member, you may have been motivated to volunteer for any of a number of reasons. Perhaps you have an abiding interest in an organization's programs, in its mission. Many people find board membership a source of personal satisfaction; they want "to give something back," to find the reward of doing a good deed. Many others volunteer for service as a way of gaining recognition in their job or in the community, and most companies encourage such participation.

A recent study of values and attitudes among the wealthy found that "the biggest status symbol among the rich is being in charge—as a trustee of a cultural or educational institution" ("Wealth in America," 1993). Achieving such a position was rated higher than being a top executive of a corporation, owning your own business, sending your children to an elite college, or owning a vacation home, expensive jewelry, or a yacht—even higher than being prominent or famous.

A Boston volunteer who received an award for her participation in community organizations commented: "There is enough of the world's work to be done that it is easy to choose a line that gives pleasure in return. . . . Volunteers have the power to effect change, to make decisions, to go directly to the pressure points; the power to ask sticky questions and to spotlight crucial facts" (Lydia Goodhue, personal communication, 1985).

Many communities have agencies whose function is to help organizations recruit volunteers, including board members, and perhaps that is where you first became interested. But it's more likely that your introduction to board membership came from a friend or associate.

If you are already volunteering your time as a board member, recruit a friend to share the pleasures. If not, get aboard and find the rewards.

Welcome to the board.

2

The Qualities of a Good Board Member

Not everyone makes a good trustee. It takes a certain mix of personal qualities and character traits, as well as skills and experience. The personal qualities are especially hard to measure. Certainly everyone has difficulty assessing his or her own qualities; it requires great openness and humility.

To begin to get a sense of these critical personal qualities, look at successful and happy board members. They tackle with relish important and often complex problems of public interest. They take an orderly approach to decision making. They are willing to deal with difficulties yet roll with frustrations. They aren't stuck on winning every issue. They are team players.

Without question, all successful board members must possess two essential qualities: *integrity* and an *open mind*.

Board members must be people of principle. On a board, any appearance of shady or slick dealings is altogether out of the question. Any conflict of interest, actual or perceived, is troublesome in deliberations and potentially damaging to the organization.

The best trustees bring to the table neither their prejudices nor their own agendas. Instead they come with a broad perspective and a willingness to search out solutions. They know that the problems they will face are complex and the solutions are not easy; often their only choice is the least flawed of several imperfect options.

Another key component is *competence*. Board members of non-profit organizations are often recruited for their expertise in a certain area, and when this is the case, clearly their level of competence in that area is especially important. But even when this is not the case, the best board members are usually competent, efficient, bright people.

A very welcome attribute, sometimes overlooked, is a *sense of humor*. People who take themselves and life too seriously are not inspiring to be around, and even boring. More to the point, their outlook can be troublesome when the board faces a difficult decision or a complex task.

Karl Mathiasen (1968), a well-known Washington, D.C., consultant to nonprofits, suggested some personality types that nonprofit organizations will be happy *not* to have on their boards:

The "Johnny-one-note," obsessed with a single issue

The devil's advocate, who persists in taking the contrary view just for show

The authority figure, accustomed to commanding and uncomfortable with group decisions

The "off-the-wall-artist," a self-centered individual who raises problems in order to give speeches on them, who has an opinion on everything but seldom has done his homework

The "board hopper," who sits on many boards but serves none

And in many ways, the most important quality of all may be *enthusiasm*. Genuine warmth and eagerness for the cause will go a long way in making a good board member; their absence is deadening.

Ralph Waldo Emerson once wrote,

Enthusiasm is one of the most powerful engines of success. When you do a thing, do it with all your might. Put your whole soul into it. Stamp it with your own personality. Be active, be energetic, be enthusiastic and faithful, and you will accomplish your object. Nothing great was ever accomplished without enthusiasm.

3

· ·

What You Should Know About the Law
Governing Nonprofits

Some of the legal paraphernalia related to establishing an organization you need to know, but a lot you don't have to bother with. You should, however, become familiar with the basics of *incorporation*, *bylaws*, and *taxes*.

Incorporation

Most nonprofit organizations are chartered as corporations by a state government, usually the state attorney general. Some, from generations ago, were created as unincorporated trusts, governed by trustees with somewhat different powers and duties. In either case, it takes a lawyer to get the organization legally founded.

While the precise nature of the articles of incorporation varies, state by state, in essence they all should contain a simple statement of the purpose of the organization and indicate how it will be governed. As a trustee you should read the articles of incorporation but otherwise not be concerned; the organization's legal counsel will deal with the chartering responsibilities.

Nonprofit organizations other than religious congregations fall into one of two categories: public service organizations created for

---

This book cannot serve as, or substitute for, legal counsel. For further information on the legal aspects of nonprofit organizations, see *Guidebook for Directors of Nonprofit Corporations* (Overton, 1993), from which much of this chapter is drawn.

the benefit of the public, and membership organizations created for the mutual benefit of the members. This seemingly tidy distinction, however, is in many ways blurred.

Membership associations, for instance, often create subordinate, separately chartered foundations or institutes to carry out programs for the benefit of the general public, not simply their own members. This practice is quite common with professional and trade associations; however, offering such public programs does not make them public service organizations.

In a reverse situation, public service organizations often establish what they refer to as memberships to hold the loyalty of supporters, often with token benefits. That move doesn't make them membership organizations. Sometimes, too, public service organizations have charters that call for a roster of members who have no governance role save that of electing the trustees. Their status as a public service does not change. The key point you should look for is whether the organization is in business to serve the public or to serve its members.

Be sure you are clear on this often-confused distinction between public service and membership organizations.

The governing boards of public service charitable organizations are generally self-perpetuating bodies; that is, they elect their own members. While legally the state attorney general can call them to account for breaches of duty, in a fiduciary sense these board members answer to the general public, to the people they serve, to their contributors, and to their own consciences.

Governing boards of membership organizations, on the other hand, are selected by the members and are accountable to them. True membership organizations present little difficulty in their governance; the board of trustees, or governors, is chosen by the members and takes action to serve the membership.

Bylaws

The bylaws go one step beyond the articles of incorporation. They define how the organization is to be governed in accordance with its own articles and the statutes. Bylaws exist to reflect the wishes of the board, not to constrain it. A board decides what kind of board it wants to be, in size and composition, and how it wants to organize itself. The board can always change its bylaws when it sees a better way of governing the organization.

Bylaws are best when they are kept simple. They do not have to spell out every detail of structure and procedure.

As a board member you should be thoroughly familiar with the bylaws; you will follow them, but don't think of them as immutable.

Taxes

Since exemption from taxes is important to any nonprofit organization, you will need to understand something about tax law. But it is a technical field and tax laws change; you don't have to become the tax expert.

Most nonprofit organizations are exempt from federal and state income tax, local property tax, and from most sales taxes on things they buy, although they must themselves collect the sales tax on items they sell (tickets, for instance). In addition, contributions made by supporters, within certain limits, are tax deductible by the donor.

Tax exemption is not a right but a privilege granted by law to organizations that meet the requirements of the Internal Revenue Code or state statutes. The Internal Revenue Code lists twenty-five types of tax-exempt organizations, including social welfare, veterans' organizations, and employee pension funds. The most numerous are nonprofit organizations operated exclusively for charitable, religious, educational, literary, artistic, or scientific purposes that qualify under the 501(c)(3) section. To qualify, an organization must not carry on substantial activities to influence legislation—lobbying—and must not participate in any way in political campaigns.

Although an organization can earn revenues through its programs, it will be subject to tax on substantial income derived from an unrelated business. Your tax expert should flag this danger. And all tax-exempt organizations with annual incomes of $25,000 or more (other than religious congregations) must file with the Internal Revenue Service a Form 990 tax return. These 990 forms call for basic financial information on the organization and the names and salaries of trustees and top officials. The 990 reports must be available to the public on request.

Unfortunately, a surprising number of organizations fail to fill out the required 990 form, and others are reluctant to make them available when requested.

The so-called watchdog organizations that review charitable organizations for conformity to standards, notably the National Charities Information Bureau and the Philanthropic Advisory Service of the Council of Better Business Bureaus, and the media, make extensive use of the information reported in the 990 forms.

Independent grant-making foundations, company-sponsored foundations, and community foundations are required to file a special form, "990 PF" (Private Foundation). The Foundation Center libraries in New York, Washington, Cleveland, and San Francisco, and cooperating collections in several other cities keep microfiche files of 990 PFs; they can be especially valuable to organizations researching sources of grants.

The privilege of tax exemption should be guarded and not abused. As a board member you should be familiar with the 990 form, be sure it is submitted by the organization, and that it is available to the public on request. It's a good idea for the board, or at least the finance committee of the board, to review the 990 regularly.

4

· ·

A Nonprofit Is Not a Business

A word of caution: don't try to uncritically apply business practices and the governance structure of for-profit companies to nonprofit organizations. When a charitable organization begins to judge itself exclusively by its business practices, it may lose sight of its primary purpose—public service.

In joining a nonprofit organization you enter an arena quite different from business. Commercial companies exist to make money. Their people, top to bottom, public-spirited and generous as they may be, are paid to deliver products and services at the lowest cost and offer them at the best prices.

When companies make generous contributions to worthy causes, they look beyond their genuine philanthropic motive to the benefits that will accrue to them, either through improved conditions in the community or through favorable notice that will be taken of their gift—or both. They must not do otherwise. Good citizenship is good business.

For-profit companies live by sales. Their performance is, quite properly, judged by the bottom line, which can be precisely measured. Nonprofit organizations, on the other hand, are judged on the good they do, for which no exact measure exists.

This distinction between for-profit and not-for-profit becomes blurred when a major part of a nonprofit's program service is something offered for sale (or otherwise reimbursed), rather than being donated. Thus universities live by tuitions, hospitals by service charges, museums and theaters by paid admissions. These public services must be handled much like a business. They are competitive. They are advertised and promoted. With earned revenues that may be figured in millions of dollars, they must operate within the strictures of business and exhibit corporate characteristics, including a close eye on the bottom line.

Large nonprofit institutions that have a strong focus on revenue earning put a special and difficult responsibility on their boards. Although the success of the institution depends on promoting its services and on rigorous cost management, much like a business, nonetheless it is not a business. It's a tax-exempt organization, and its board has an obligation to assure that it fulfills its public service mission. The organization exists to serve people, not to reap profits.

Board members of most nonprofit organizations—that is, other than the larger institutions and other than those that derive most of their income from earned revenues—need constantly to focus attention on attracting contributed funds to carry out programs. As a board member of one of these smaller institutions, you will not be faced with maximizing earned revenues and a total absorption with the bottom line.

Nevertheless, as a board member of either kind of organization, one dependent on earned revenues or one dependent on contributed income, you will want to define precisely what service is needed and then whether it is being performed well, with financial responsibility. The task is not easy. As attorney and management consultant Christopher Hodgkin points out, "What is clear is that measuring success in the nonprofit organization is much more subjective than in the business corporation, and involves directors making subjective personal judgments to a much greater degree than is the case of a corporate board" (1993).

Another frequently overlooked difference between the operations of business and nonprofit organizations is in decision making. In business, when management makes a decision, that's it; it is carried out. The implementing action may take time, and hurdles may need to be overcome, but management is virtually in full control from start to finish.

Not so with charitable organizations. Management has no such clear command authority. Many constituencies must be taken into account. Consider, for example, educational institutions: making and implementing decisions involves—aside from administration officials—faculties, students, parents, alumni, members of the community where the institution is located, and possibly affiliated institutions. Similarly with hospitals, or community service organizations: many people, directly or indirectly connected, are in the act.

A part of the problem may be the word *businesslike*, as in "You/we should be more businesslike in our operation." To a businessperson, *businesslike* means being strong, being professional in determining costs, and especially being conscious of profit and loss. To a manager of a nonprofit organization, being businesslike means monitoring costs versus benefits, not profit versus loss. Being diligent and expert in determining costs of programs is of course a paramount concern, but that by itself doesn't mean the organization is businesslike. What counts in nonprofit management is cost/benefit.

The emphasis on being businesslike probably stems from the fact that charitable organizations have had to overcome a widespread reputation that they are managed by soft do-gooders unwilling to face financial facts. If it was ever valid, this reputation has taken a long time dying. One observer has suggested: "The myth of corporate superiority over nonprofits is fueled by the fact that corporations can generally cover over their mistakes unless they hit the headlines, while nonprofits do most of their business in the sunshine with many onlookers and critics" (Merchant, 1990).

As a board member you should note well that a basic difference between business and philanthropic organizations shows up in their governance structure. Boards of corporations, answering as they do to their owners—the stockholders—tend to be small and efficient. They are called upon to make broad policy decisions. Their members, chosen for their competence, are usually paid handsomely.

Nonprofit boards, on the other hand, tend to be larger and, by business standards, not efficient. Because they are answerable to the public, nonprofit boards benefit from diversity of membership and representation of many constituencies. The well-run board of a non-profit organization seeks competent members but also looks for those who bring special skills (legal, accounting, public relations, fundraising) as well as detailed experience in the organization's field—arts, education, social work. Unlike corporate boards, these disparate, unpaid members of nonprofit boards are responsible for seeing that the programs are useful and well run, and for attracting contributed funds sufficient to carry out the service mission.

Nonprofit boards should, and do, welcome the hard-nosed, problem-solving acumen of the business world. Business leaders well versed in financial matters can be enormously helpful; they are often the strongest members of a philanthropic board. As leading members of the community they are probably the major participants in the fundraising effort. On the other hand, William G. Bowen, president of the Andrew W. Mellon Foundation and former president of Princeton University, asks the question, "Is it true that well-regarded representatives of the business world are often surprisingly ineffective as members of nonprofit boards?" He answers his own question thus:

> Although it would be difficult to devise a rigorous empirical test, I suspect that my harsh-sounding proposition questioning the effectiveness of nonprofit board members from the business sector holds with surprising frequency. This impression is certainly widely shared—by many business executives, among others [Bowen, 1994].

In any event, caution is called for when a nonprofit board is faced with a strong push to allow business criteria to dominate matters of governance and program management. When asked, "Why don't you run this place like a business?" say, "Because it's not a business; it's a public service."

These differences and similarities between commercial and philanthropic enterprises may affect you as a board member. You may be called upon to make decisions that are similar to those facing a business, but never forget that the fundamental purpose of your organization is public service.

• • • • • • •

You hear a lot about the need for nonprofits to do a better job of marketing; should board members get involved?
"Marketing" is a good example. You need to be careful when applying business terms and practices uncritically to nonprofit organizations. The concept of marketing a public service may seem like a good idea on the surface, but it can easily bring serious confusion.

Start with a basic distinction. Markets are a function of the free enterprise system where goods and services are produced and sold to make money, at a price where supply and demand meet. Nonprofit institutions exist to provide services for the common good, for advocacy, or for mutual benefit. Earned revenue may be an important source of income, but nonprofits depend, usually in significant measure, on contributions.

Thus, in business you have "customers"—people to whom you want to sell a product or service; they are the ones who constitute your market. In nonprofit services, instead of customers you have three quite different kinds of "constituents." One constituency is the recipients of the service, whoever they are—the homeless, the sick, troubled children, the world at large. Clearly, you don't sell—that is, market—these nonpaying beneficiaries.

Another constituency is the contributors who support the public service by their grants and donations. Some people say that marketing is the way to make fundraising dollars more productive, to find big donors and build stronger relationships with them. But do you really "sell" a wing of the hospital to the donor who wants to honor a deceased spouse? Though benefits are given and received, charitable donations are simply not bought and sold. Of course you diligently and expertly research prospective donors—individuals, companies, foundations, United Ways, and other grant-making organizations. And you cultivate prospective donors in the sense of gaining their interest and involvement. But it is a stretch to relate these activities to the business concept of marketing.

The third constituency, the one that comes closest to the concept of consumers to be marketed, is those who pay to receive a public service: museum goers, university students, hospice patients. In the competition for those paying for the service, organizations do have to analyze carefully who needs the services, how the services can be made most attractive, at what cost. And they may have to advertise and promote the services.

Is that marketing? There is a fine line here. You may see those activities as "selling" the services to this third group and therefore these constituents are "customers" to be "marketed." That view does, however, seem somewhat to disregard the basic public service purpose of the institution.

A major part of the problem is getting people to define with any precision what they mean by *marketing*. If, as people often do, you simply mean promotion, then say so. Enthusiastic academics and practitioners pressing to apply marketing techniques to nonprofit organizations seem to attribute to "marketing" most of what is essentially effective management—intelligently, aggressively, and innovatively planning, seeing what services are needed, who needs them, and how the programs can most effectively be carried out and promoted to serve them.

The central point for you as a board member is this: accept the similarity to business practices of some nonprofit activities and the need to learn many things from business, but don't let them overwhelm what your organization is really about. The job of the board is to assure that the fundamental public service of the organization prevails, that it is performed well, even aggressively, and in a financially responsible manner.

"On the contrary, I do feel that our marriage still works,
we just have to start marketing it differently."

Part II

. . . .

Board Member Responsibilities

5

· ·

Your Role as a Board Member

You will ask yourself, Am I qualified? Or, more directly, What really is expected of me as a trustee, and will I fulfill that expectation? If you are already a board member, it is, Am I fulfilling the expectation?

No two boards are the same. Because organizations differ widely in size, in structure, and particularly in their purpose and reason for existence, their boards are bound to be different in character and ways of operation. Boards of national organizations will differ from those of community organizations. Certainly, too, the problems and opportunities facing different boards will vary enormously. But, remarkably, what is expected of a trustee—the basic responsibilities of a board member—will not vary substantially.

The thesis of this book is simply stated: What is expected of a trustee of a nonprofit organization can be summarized in seven quite specific responsibilities. With rarest exceptions, a board member is expected to fulfill all seven. They are listed here and described in detail in the succeeding chapters.

Your role as a trustee has two aspects: fiduciary and supportive. As a representative of the public at large you have a fiduciary obligation to watch out for the public interest. Your supportive role is to help make the organization work, to assist it in achieving its mission. All seven responsibilities of a board member fall into one or both of these purposes.

The seven responsibilities are set out in the following list and discussed in succeeding chapters. Such a summary list will be of value in recruiting new members and assuring they know what is expected of them. Because the seven will also be important in board self-assessments, discussed in Chapter Twelve, they are presented here in Exhibit 5.1 and in checklist form in Exhibit 12.1.

Exhibit 5.1. Seven Responsibilities of a Board Member.

1. *Attendance.* To attend board meetings and participate in some committee work

2. *Mission.* To define the mission and participate periodically in *strategic planning* to review purposes, programs, priorities, funding needs, and targets of achievement

3. *Chief executive.* To approve the selection, compensation, and, if necessary, dismissal of the chief executive and assure regular evaluation of the executive's performance

4. *Finances.* To assure financial responsibility by:

    Approving the annual *budget* and overseeing adherence to it

    Contracting for an independent *audit*

    Controlling the *investment* policies and management of capital or reserve funds

5. *Program oversight and support.* To oversee and evaluate all programs, support the staff, and be an advocate in the community

6. *Fundraising.* To contribute personally and annually and participate in identification, cultivation, and solicitation of prospective supporters

7. *Board effectiveness.* To assure the board fulfills the foregoing governance responsibilities and maintains effective organization, procedures, and recruitment

While the responsibilities of a board member will not vary significantly with boards of different sizes and kinds, the manner in which board members deal with the responsibilities can differ considerably. The maturity of an organization and the culture, the individual personality of its board, will affect how board members handle their role.

Take first the matter of maturity. One analysis of organizational growth (Knauft, Berger, and Gray, 1991) identifies three stages:

1. *Startup*, characterized by a small group of volunteers, or a single highly motivated individual, responding to a cause or problem. Goals tend to be subjective, and a "can-do" spirit pervades. The major challenges are in formalizing the structure and raising funds.

2. *Growth*, characterized by some stability and probably a full-time executive director and staff. The principal challenges are keeping up the momentum, maintaining the funding base, and diversifying the board.

3. *Maturity*, where the organization has reached a degree of stability and self-sufficiency, and has developed a credible track record.

As organizations reach maturity, its board will confront various challenges:

• Weaning members away from involvement in operations and management they had become used to

• Keeping a large, prestigious board committed and active

• Ensuring that the organization does not become purely staff driven

• Addressing the needs and problems of a large staff

• Recognizing the need for self-renewal among staff and board, including bringing aboard new people and new ideas

Once again, these changes and challenges are significant in the way you fulfill your responsibilities, but none dictates a different set of responsibilities expected of each board member.

The term *culture* refers to shared beliefs, underlying assumptions of how things should be done. Holland, Leslie, and Holzhalb (1993) explain: "Practices and assumptions gradually become embedded in culture. . . . As ways of doing business become habitual, . . . underlying assumptions sink into the minds of participants and come to shape the ways they perceive new issues that come to the board. These assumptions fall below conscious awareness but still organize and structure participants' responses to events. They constitute the undebatable, subliminal foundations for any action."

Thus boards can take on personality traits—open or secretive, confident or hesitant, detached or deeply involved, effective or ineffective. But regardless of differences in culture, the responsibilities of board members remain the same.

6

Attending Board Meetings

You attend board meetings, of course. As most boards have active committees, you will also serve on at least one committee, attend its meetings, and participate in its work: overseeing staff, reviewing reports, or preparing recommendations.

So what's the problem?

The problem is that some people accept trusteeships without expecting to attend and participate in meetings. Don't be one of them. Recognize from the outset that if you choose not to attend meetings, your fitness for membership is brought into question.

Occasionally—but only occasionally—it is acceptable to have a trustee who does not attend meetings. A prestigious name or reputation may burnish the organization's community image, or someone with significant financial resources may be sorely needed. For example, a prominent restaurateur declines to attend board meetings but offers his facilities for benefits and conferences; should he be continued as a trustee? Of course.

In general, however, all board members should willingly accept that meetings are part of the job, and that their whole-hearted participation is part of the responsibility.

Early notices and frequent reminders help achieve good attendance. The best assurance, though, is to see to it that meetings are well run and productive; strong leadership by the chair will keep attendance from lagging.

Your participation in committee work is also important. Many nonprofit organizations, especially small ones, have what are sometimes known as working boards, in which committees take on specific responsibilities and special projects to supplement the work done by the small staff. Even when this is not the case, board committees—budget, development, and program committees, for instance—focus the board's attention on the issues in these central functions. You should be willing to join in this effort, contributing time and attention beyond merely showing up for board meetings.

In support of this notion, the Council of Better Business Bureaus (1986) suggests you should ask yourself whether you can afford the time it takes to be an effective board member:

> In addition to attending board meetings, you should expect to spend time preparing for those meetings, serving on subcommittees, appearing at fund raising events, and contacting potential donors. . . . Evaluate your other commitments and figure out how you will find time for serving on a board. . . . It is not fair to the organization for you to agree to serve when you know you do not have enough time to do a good job. You should also be wary of lending your name and reputation to an organization you don't have time to monitor.

To protect against poor participation, some organizations establish a policy, even stipulating it in the bylaws, of removing a trustee after a specified number of unexcused absences. It rarely works. A better solution is to have a rotation in tenure; then, instead of the traumatic action of dismissal, nonattending members can simply not be reelected.

7

··

Defining the Mission
and Strategic Planning

Charitable organizations today face increasingly complex economic, social, demographic, and political environments. Their
strategic plans, their determination of vision, and the programs to
fulfill the mission will be significantly affected by changing and
hard-to-predict pressures and opportunities. They may face competition from other agencies in the same field; they may lose their
identity after a controversial merger with another organization.

Thus, with increased numbers of organizations engaged in community services, education, health care, and other public purposes,
determining the proper niche for each may not be as simple as it at first
appears. What is required is a lengthy process of soul searching and
self-assessment, in the form of strategic planning and mission setting.

It is a function of the board to establish the organization's mission and, through strategic planning, periodically to review the
mission and the programs that carry it out. As a trustee you will seek
to understand the mission, endorse it, and support it. You will probably find participation in the strategic planning process a rewarding part of your trusteeship; it will be a continuing way of knowing
and reaching deep commitment to your organization.

But don't expect unanimity of views on these matters. As management consultant Hodgkin explains, "The process of mission definition is extraordinarily complex, often fuzzy, and generally
philosophical, constituency-based, and value-oriented" (1993).

However, difficult though it may be, this is a task for the board. So important to the organization are a comprehensive definition of its mission and strategic planning, you should not turn them over to a committee or to an outside consultant. The board and staff must grapple with these complex questions. On the other hand, a board can find it useful to charge a special committee to make "plans for planning"; that is, to keep the board's attention on the need for planning and to make the arrangements for the board to fulfill its planning responsibilities. But the board must do the planning.

Defining the Mission

To begin with, what the term *mission* means can be a source of confusion. For some people a mission statement is a tidy paragraph, carefully crafted for a brochure or annual report, succinctly explaining what the organization does. Although such a statement has its uses, it does not fulfill the need to define the overall purpose and programs of the organization. The mission is therefore better understood to be a comprehensive document that sets out the board's determination of the purposes, the framework, and the bounds of the organization's activities. That document is designed for private, not public, distribution.

Such a comprehensive determination of the mission can be achieved through a planning process by which the board, preferably with staff participation, agrees on an articulation of purpose and the means of achieving that purpose.

Strategic Planning

Effective strategic planning usually starts with an exploration of two underlying elements. One is an assessment of future economic, social, demographic, and environmental trends and their possible and probable impact on the institution and its programs. Somewhat of a crystal ball, but nevertheless necessary to look into.

The other element is a thorough and realistic examination of the need for what the organization does, the *why* of its existence. From that can be developed an indisputable justification for the organization and its programs. Every institution wants to make a difference, to be able to demonstrate what happens if that need is not met. Sound planning must be built on a realistic view of what the need of the community or the nation is and a solid rationale for the organization and its programs. Even the plans of such institutions as schools, health organizations, and museums, whose purposes are usually taken for granted, are stronger if they focus first on just why they exist.

From this broad look at the environment in which an organization operates, and the underlying need for its existence, a plan can unfold, based on what will be asked of the organization in the years ahead and how it can respond appropriately.

Good planning thus makes clear the vision of what the organization wants to be and do in the coming years in light of anticipated circumstances and environment. It projects the programs it will need to undertake to fulfill that vision. Only with such a sense of purpose, and determination of programs to fulfill that purpose, can an organization fix on its priorities.

With such a statement of the mission at hand, the board can call on the staff to flesh out the several programs in greater detail, setting out for both the substantive and administrative programs:

- A simple statement of purpose: what the basic intent of the program is

- The current status: what is now being done

- Planned courses of action: what changes are to be undertaken, and when

- Targets: what points of measurable achievement, at what stated times, are set

- Administration: who is going to do what and at what added cost

You will find that once the board has assured itself of the mission—the vision and the programs to fulfill the vision—you will have a base for moving confidently forward in determining the funding needs and preparing the case for why people should support the organization. With such a comprehensive statement of the mission the board can also establish procedures to evaluate performance; without it a board lacks a basis for making judgments.

Be aware, however, that there is a different concept of the board's role in setting strategy, one that challenges the foregoing more conventional view. It holds that strategy should be composed by those charged with the responsibility for implementing it—the executive and staff—leaving to the board the function of policy approval, oversight of implementation, and funding. The rationale is that, since the board always has to be in a position to question and evaluate alternatives, it should not itself formulate the strategic plans, should not be committed to any one strategy.

This alternative view seems to have greater validity for business corporations than for nonprofits. The chief executive of a business, not the board of directors, is responsible for profit and loss. In nonprofit organizations, however, the focus is cost/benefit—and that falls squarely on the shoulders of the trustees. It is they who are responsible for the public service that the organization provides and for raising the funds to support the programs, and so—the argument goes—it is for them to determine the kinds of services and how those services will be carried out.

Make sure you know where your board stands on this matter.

It is not easy to bring boards and staffs together in the time-consuming process of strategic planning. How should you go about it? Should you hold retreats, assembling board members and staff somewhere away from phones, fax, and family? Should you use focus groups of constituents to highlight their special concerns? Should you bring in a neutral leader from outside to help you achieve useful results? What preplanning papers should you prepare? You will need to face these questions deliberately.

And expect semantic differences when people get involved in planning. More than in most managerial activities, planning terms carry varying meanings to different people. Take such common words as *objectives* and *goals*. To some, the objectives are the broad purposes, and goals are the specific targets; others reverse those meanings. *Strategies* is another loosely defined word often thrown in to cover an unclear thought. *Excellence* and *unique* have been abused; it is the rare organization that does not strive for excellence and claim to be unique. Don't let the planning process be derailed by semantic arguments.

As a conscientious board member you can accept the challenge of developing a strong mission statement and the strategic planning to achieve it. You will want to maneuver your work schedule so as to participate. Then make sure that the tough questions are not avoided: What is the real need that the organization seeks to meet, what will the organization do to meet that need, and how will it go about it?

That is true planning.

• • • • • • •

Why do so many strategic plans seem to gather dust on shelves, unused? For a number of reasons, strategic plans often fall short of expectations. The process of planning is not easy; it is difficult to bring people together and get them to produce a clear and useful document. People take cover in broad statements and fail to address the tough questions. The jargon of planning can get in the way of a good plan.

Probably the most telling reason strategic planning suffers lies in the initial approach to the task. You can't begin to talk about your vision, your programs, or your mission until and unless you have identified what is needed in the community, the nation, or the world. That is the "focus problem"—the *why* of the organization's existence that must come first; without it, statements of what the organization is going to do are meaningless.

When you worry about the value of the product, remember, President Eisenhower said that the importance of planning is not so much in the plan itself as in the process of preparing it—the effort and thinking that goes into it.

Careful preparation for the planning process is absolutely essential. It is too easy, for instance, to underestimate the demands on those who will be leading the planning sessions. Time is limited, issues are many, and strong views are usually rampant. For a useful document to emerge, discussion must be directed and the content of discussions captured.

Don't go for length. Shorter plans are more likely to come to grips with key issues than are plans that go into great detail, trying to cover every base. It takes longer and is more demanding to prepare a short document that gets to the heart of the issues, but the outcome is surely more valuable.

If the essential components of the vision of the organization's future are agreed, and the several programs to carry it out clearly identified, a plan can be a living document, guiding the board in its governance and directing management in implementation.

8

Choosing and Evaluating the Chief Executive

No more important or sensitive task confronts you as a trustee than selecting a new chief executive—unless it's dismissing the current executive.

Fortunately, the task of selecting a new chief executive arises only occasionally. When it does, it immediately becomes the dominant item on the board's agenda.

The Selection Process

You will want to do your part to assure that both the search and the selection are handled with the greatest care and sensitivity. You will want to assure, too, that the appropriate amount of time is devoted to this task. Don't allow the process to become rushed with an artificial deadline. You want to move along on a deliberate, but not rigid, schedule. Either delay or forcing a deadline presents dangers.

When the executive vacancy occurs, the first job for the board is to be explicit on the qualities and competencies it wants in a new manager. As organizations grow and evolve, different strengths need to be brought to staff leadership. The executive is at the heart of the organization, and so the board must spell out the qualities and expertise needed by the organization as it is today. It is dangerous to look for exactly what you had, and even more dangerous to rely on the generality that you will "look for the best person."

It is without doubt a difficult process. Do not be ashamed if you feel awed by the complexities of the search and selection. Subjective judgments are intensified when selecting such a key player in the organization, and even when an insider is a clear-cut candidate for promotion to the top spot, you will face a wide selection of candidates.

A change in the chief executive is an excellent time for a complete review of the organizational mission, for confirming strategic plans, for envisioning what the organization wants to be in the coming years. Only after emerging from this process is the board truly ready to charge a search committee with its assignment. Defining the vision and the qualifications are jobs for the board, not for the search committee.

Boards establish search committees to seek out, interview, recommend, and obtain references for candidates. However, without precise instructions from the board, search committees can run into difficulties. Clear instructions can guard against a common hazard: a committee so committed to a single candidate that it preempts the board's decision. A diligent board will direct the search committee to recommend one, or two, or even three candidates, perhaps in the committee's order of preference, but in any event to recommend viable candidates they will stand behind. Then the board is free to deliberate and decide on one. The board, not the committee, has to live with the chosen executive.

Establishing the executive's role is a delicate matter. Personalities, sensitivities, and confidentiality are all involved. Yet having a sound relationship between the board and executive makes for success, and its opposite leads to failure. Experience and alertness on the part of the board members are the only assurances. You will want to support the executive until it is demonstrable that you cannot. And then strong resolve is called for.

Evaluating the Executive's Job Performance

Another key board task in this area is evaluating on a regular basis the performance and effectiveness of the executive. It may be helpful to think of the board, the executive, and the staff as three entities. As is discussed in greater detail in Chapter Ten, the board holds the executive responsible for management, including hiring, paying, supervising, evaluating, and dismissing the staff. In its governance role, the board itself, and you as an individual board member, should scrupulously avoid any interference with the executive's exercise of that authority over the staff, even when circumstances seem to invite it.

The board must evaluate the executive, yet obviously the whole board cannot participate in this sensitive area. The board can and should put a specific evaluation process in place. Some organizations have found it effective to establish a small committee with the sole function of carrying out this process. A "personnel committee" is not the appropriate vehicle, for it deals with personnel policy and employee grievance appeals—altogether different from executive evaluation. Nor is it wise to have the board chair lead the executive evaluation; the relationship between the chair and the executive, intrinsic to executive effectiveness and yet always one that is evolving, must itself be evaluated.

Fixing the executive's salary is particularly sensitive. In some cases a contract, yearly or multiyear, may be desirable. Because contract negotiation can introduce distracting elements to the evaluation process, the two should be kept separate, both in time and in committee assignment. Although organizations often want to keep the executive's salary confidential, in fact it becomes public when IRS Form 990 is filed.

When carried out annually and constructively, the evaluation process can prove helpful to both the executive and the board. It can be most effective when based on the executive's own plan for the year with its targets and dates for achievement of them. Executives prepare such plans for their own purposes and then share them with the board.

When that sensitive and unhappy time comes to dismiss an executive, this too must be a decision of the full board, not a committee. You can readily see that dangers will arise when this decision is made by a faction of the board. Moreover, it is impossible to fire someone in a manner satisfactory to all parties. Board members must ready themselves to counter the usual but unhelpful critic who says, "The decision to dismiss was understandable, but the way it was done was wrong." Try, if at all possible, to work out amicable, and preferably confidential, arrangements for a parting.

As a board member you will do well to be aware of and sensitive to all these matters, even when others on the board may appear to be more qualified to deal with them. You contribute much when you insist on fair and effective action in the board's relationship with its executive, from definition of function to selection and contract with the successor.

. . . .

Should the executive be a voting member of the board?
More importance is attached to this question than it probably deserves. Chief executives normally sit with the board as ex officio members; the question is whether they should be full voting members.

The case for the affirmative asserts that full voting board membership gives executives a more collegial, peer relationship with the other board members that may help them to be more effective. The chief executives of large national organizations, universities and colleges, and major hospitals, customarily have the prestigious title of president; that entitles them to full board membership.

This advantage, especially in smaller organizations, is probably more perceived than real. Some, for instance, think it is helpful in fundraising. However, if executive directors are competent, they probably don't need voting membership to reinforce their performance.

The case for the negative points to the responsibility of boards to hire, pay, evaluate performance of, and if necessary dismiss the executives. In this respect the executive, as the servant of the board, is in an ambiguous position and should not participate as a voting member.

A 1994 report (Independent Sector) points out that while six of ten executive officers serve on the board, only approximately half have voting membership.

Little seems to be gained, and some confusion and perhaps difficulty arise, when the executive sits on the board other than ex officio.

9

. . . .

Assuring Financial Responsibility

Nonprofit organizations are often criticized for their handling of finances—some of it thoroughly deserved. Indeed, criticism has been appropriately laid on organizations that allowed sudden deficits or based their budgets on fundraising hopes rather than funds on hand. You as a board member must be constantly alert to ensure that the organization is handling its finances responsibly.

You may think of yourself as being "innumerate"—unable to deal with numbers. But even if accounting is not your field, and even though some number-crunching trustees seem to hold the role of financial watchdogs, you can still have an impact. Don't be afraid to ask questions. Satisfy yourself that you understand the figures and accept their validity—or at least that others whom you respect can accept them.

As part of the task of overseeing the finances of the organization and maintaining financial controls, the board monitors financial statements. The staff keeps the books and manages the accounts. The board, usually acting through a finance committee, must assure itself that the finances are in order. "Order" in this case means two things: financial integrity and financial performance.

Integrity is clear-cut; it is either there or not there. On the other hand, performance—meaning whether or not the organization is on a sound financial footing—can be difficult to evaluate. It's the nature of nonprofit organizations to struggle financially.

Emeritus Harvard Business School professor and former Colby College board chair Robert Anthony offers these guidelines: "The financial performance of a nonprofit organization is satisfactory if, on average, the organization at least breaks even. In some years, the organization may generate a reasonable amount of net income to provide working capital and a cushion against future rainy days. In other years, a net loss is tolerated. If the organization consistently generates large surpluses, there is an indication that it has not provided the quantity of services that clients, grantors, contributors, and other supporters have a right to expect. If it consistently generates losses, the organization will go bankrupt (1991).

In terms of both integrity and performance, as a responsible trustee you will need to deal with three aspects of financial affairs: the *budget*, the *audit*, and *investments* of capital or reserve funds. These are separate matters; the fact that all three relate to money should not lead you to see them as functionally the same. Nor can responsibility for them be relegated to the staff, or to one or two trustees nimble with numbers. A separate board committee can assume most of the burden of dealing with each of these functions, focusing the board's attention, but ultimately they are responsibilities for the full board.

The Budget

You should look on the budget process as having a dual purpose. It is, first, a control document, the mechanism by which the board assures that the organization operates within its means, that programs and projects are not undertaken unless the money to pay for them is available. Second, the budget is a policy and planning document, the instrument by which the board decides what the organization will do and how it will do it. The budget determines the direction and extent of the organization's activities.

But, as management consultant John Carver points out, "budget approval and control lies at the interface of board governance and staff management" (1991). In dealing with the budget, boards must fulfill their control responsibility but not cross over into management by seeking to direct a program through the budget process. The temptation may be great, for it is the one clear path boards have to enter operations. They must resist. Boards select the executive for the precise purpose of managing the operations.

Budget presentations, prepared by budget committees with assistance from the executive and staff, can be most helpful when they identify and highlight the essential issues that deserve board consideration. It is not only the numbers that count: the policy implications invariably imbedded in the budget determine the direction the organization's activities take.

Remember, too, that budgets are part of a process: they come before the board at various stages during the year for review and change as conditions warrant. On the other hand, Carver also cautions that "having a budget on the table can seduce otherwise large-minded people to become trivial" (1991). When carefully led, a board discussion of the budget grapples with policy changes and fundraising challenges; it does not get mired in mere numbers.

Audits

Be sure that contracting for an independent audit remains with the board and is not taken over by the executive or a member of the staff. The audit is the irreplaceable instrument for assuring financial accuracy and honesty. Although certified public accountants will of course need to relate closely to the finance staff and the executive, no one should doubt that the auditors are the agents of the board and report to it.

Trustees not comfortable with financial statements can find audits enigmatic and frustrating. The audit never seems to jibe with what the board faces in spreadsheets throughout the year. Audits seem to be ancient history, showing up when you are well into next year's operations.

It is possible, though, to make audits immensely helpful. Although the auditors' mandate calls upon them to report only that the finances are "free of material misstatements," auditors can be asked to identify financial and administrative procedures that need examination or could be improved. Like other professional consultants, auditors bring to their task the perspective of experience with other like organizations. You can benefit from their informal counsel. But you must request it. Although this opportunity to get the most benefit from the auditors is usually left to the board treasurer or chair of the finance committee, other members can make sure the benefit is not overlooked.

Investments

Board responsibility for handling investments of all capital and reserve funds is quite different from dealing with budgets and other financial matters. It is one of the few areas where the board has a managerial role. Specifically, the board:

- Defines the investment portfolio policies, setting guidelines for investment to balance the goals of growth or income and determining the mix of equity and debt instruments.

- Selects an independent investment management agency to handle the investments in accordance with those policies, and monitors closely the managing agent's performance.

- Governs the amount of investment returns that will be available for the operational budget.

As a trustee you can ensure that agencies selected to handle the investments are given direction—an investment policy to govern the decisions the agency will take. Also be sure they are closely monitored; agents should know that their every move is being watched and evaluated, and that changes will be made if their performance doesn't come up to scratch.

Usually a board will want to have an investment committee, quite separate from any budget or audit committee, to focus on these critical matters.

These three aspects of financial control—budgets, audits, and investments—are such key parts of the board's responsibilities as to command your close attention. Whether you are a numbers person or not, just make sure the staff and your board colleagues present the issues intelligibly to you and you will be doing a service.

* * * * * * *

Does size matter?
It is in the matter of financial responsibility of boards that you find the biggest difference between the large national and the smaller community organizations. All need to watch the finances carefully, but, as recent public disclosures have highlighted, it is the multimillion-dollar organizations with highly paid executives, plush expense accounts, and huge investment portfolios that are vulnerable to mismanagement, conflicts of interest, or unethical and illegal actions.

Watchdog agencies, investigative media, and regulators have a sharp eye out. As a board member of one of these major organizations you have every reason to be especially careful and alert, to pay strict attention to board members' financial responsibility. But if you are a trustee of a local independent school or community service organization, your problems are probably more concerned with removing deficits than with financial malfeasance. You are more aware of underpaying than overpaying your staff.

Nevertheless, the ultimate financial responsibility for both kinds of organizations remains the same—with the board.

10

. . . .

Supporting and Overseeing Programs

A trustee is called upon both to support the executive and staff, and to oversee staff performance and fulfillment of the mission. The two functions are complementary.

You will probably find that your support of the executive and staff is more important to their morale than you might have thought. Hard-working staff members are stronger knowing that board members understand their needs and stand behind them.

Board members contribute much when they support the program in public. It helps when board members are known in the community for their association with the organization and therefore their endorsement of its programs. Whether formally or informally, board members become advocates for the organization.

Board member participation in fundraising is covered in the next chapter. But there are many other ways you can help the executive or a staff member deal with specific problems (whether administrative or programmatic), especially when a public or publicity dimension is involved.

The difficult problem arises in defining the board's oversight responsibilities. In the dynamic of nonprofit operations, simple, realistic, viable lines of demarcation between the executive's management role and the board's governance role are hard to draw, as you will repeatedly find. The problem is highlighted in the budget process discussed in the preceding chapter. It is one thing to oversee administrative programs—finances, property management, personnel policies—but quite another to oversee the substantive programs—medical care, social work, educational curriculum, artistic production. Where does oversight end and controlling the program begin? It is frequently a tough call and always sensitive.

The board looks to its chief executive to select, direct, and evaluate the performance of all subordinate staff. That much is clear. But the concept of board governance implies the exercise of authority over the actions of the organization. Executive management, on the other hand, refers to the execution, the implementation, the conduct of the affairs of the organization in pursuit of the mission under the board's policy direction. Those definitions present a dangerously unclear line.

Individual decisions of an executive can impinge upon policy and thus modify the overall board-established direction. On the other hand, board decisions, especially in the details of budget approvals, can encroach on management operations.

Experienced leaders have set out interesting views on the subject of governance and management. Richard Lyman, former president of Stanford University and of the Rockefeller Foundation, has this perspective on the board-staff relationship:

> Much ink and rhetoric has been spilled over the question of establishing a clear demarcation between the board's role and that of the [executive]. It is customary to place the dividing line between management (the [executive's] responsibility) and policy making (the governing board's responsibility). . . . I find it more useful to emphasize the question of initiative. A board seldom can make policy from the ground up; it is more likely to be asked to respond to [executive] initiatives in policy making by approving, modifying, or rejecting proposals put before it [1985].

The Council of Better Business Bureaus makes a different point:

A board that insists on having a hand in virtually every decision will impede progress rather than enhance it. The board must believe in the staff and trust that it will make decisions on a day-to-day basis consistent with the overall purpose of the organization. It is crucial that board and staff maintain a good working relationship to produce the results that donors desire [1986].

Management guru Peter Drucker has still another outlook on the subject:

What are the respective tasks of the board and the executive officer? The conventional answer is that the board makes policy and the executive officer executes it. The trouble with this elegant answer is that no one knows (or has ever known) what policy is, let alone where its boundaries lie. As a result, there is constant wrangling, constant turf battles, constant friction [1990].

A common cliché warns boards to stay out of management; they should have a "watchful eye," not a "meddling hand." Again, Peter Drucker has a different perspective:

Boards should meddle. To begin with, there is no way to stop them, and if you can't lick them, you had better join them! Board members of nonprofit organizations should be committed to the cause. They should be deeply interested and involved in it, they should know the programs and the people who work on them and they should *care*. But also, nonprofit boards are usually organized in such a way that "meddling" is part of their job. They work in committees, each with a specific mandate, such as fund raising, or physical facilities, or youth activities. This forces them to work directly—that is, without going though the executive officer—with people working in

the particular area of the committee's concern. It thus
forces them to "meddle." They had better be organized
to meddle constructively [1990].

The important point is that boards in their meddling must avoid
usurping the executive's responsibility for management decisions.
They must stay clear of micromanagement, which means getting
too deeply into details. This mandate applies to interference in
either programs or administration, except that boards must take a
prominent part in budgeting and fundraising.

As a trustee you are consistently treading between meddling and
rubber stamping. The board must guard against delegating to the
executive decisions that are governance in nature. You will want to
be watchful in this area of potential confusion, and to recognize,
acknowledge, and deal with significant encroachments on the part
of either board or staff.

Two situations involving board oversight and relations with the
executive can be particularly difficult. A board chair, especially
someone not otherwise fully occupied, can find a nonprofit organization to be a sandbox in which to play, causing difficulties for the
executive. A good chair will keep in close touch and be supportive,
but guard against intruding.

Board–executive relations can also be put to strain when a
trustee has a problem with a member of the staff. The board member should refer the matter to the executive or the chair and avoid
at all costs any direct action toward the staff member.

Looked at positively, as a trustee you appreciate the role of the
executive and deal with it understandingly and sensitively. It is
healthy for both board and executive to recognize one overall guide-
line: while the distinction between governance and management
may be imprecise, in every disagreement on what is the board's
responsibility and what is the executive's, the board, not the executive, makes the decision.

. . . .

11

Participating in Fundraising

I n almost all you do as a board member, you are deliberating and deciding; in fundraising, however, you are participating. Note this distinction well, because fundraising calls upon you to play a more active part than in most of your other board responsibilities.

To understand the board member's role in fundraising, you need to be clear first about *where the responsibility lies,* and then about *what a trustee can do.* You should also be alert to the special problems associated with *raising capital funds* and *oversight responsibilities* that go with fundraising.

Who Is Responsible

Responsibility for attracting resources lies with the board. It cannot pass on to anyone else the responsibility for the resources to sustain the programs—not to the staff, not to a committee, not to an outside consultant or agent.

It is true that some health care and educational institutions create foundations to raise contributed funds, usually in order to separate donated money from government appropriations or reimbursements. In the end, however, the board of the institution stands

---

Some of the concepts in this chapter are drawn from *The Board Member's Guide to Fund Raising* by Fisher Howe (San Francisco: Jossey-Bass, 1991).

responsible for the success or failure of the foundation's fundraising effort. Boards of other public service organizations sometimes consider setting up a separate organization to do the unwelcome work of fundraising, or they think about hiring someone to raise money for them. But they too cannot remove themselves from the ultimate responsibility.

However, it is equally important to recognize that the board is helpless in fulfilling its responsibility without strong staff support. Rarely if ever can a board by itself raise all the money required to support the programs.

Accept therefore that fundraising must be a partnership of board and staff. In no other way can it work. Neither board nor staff can succeed without the other. Accordingly, the key is to put attention on the roles of each, defining what the staff and what the board should do in the fundraising effort.

The staff must always keep the files, records, and mailing lists. The staff does the research so essential to successful fundraising. And the staff prepares correspondence, acknowledgments of donations, and proposals that seek the support of foundations, corporations, or government agencies.

Fundraising, as with any program, needs to be planned. Preparing thorough program plans for raising money is clearly part of the staff role. Such plans can be discussed with a board development committee and, if brought before the board for approval, can help assure participation of all members. To be most helpful, a fundraising plan should identify the various sources or fundraising projects, and for each set out a plan with the following components: (1) the basic purpose of the project, (2) what is currently being done, (3) what is planned for the future, (4) specific targets of achievement, and (5) administration—who is responsible and how much it will cost. Presented in this fashion, such a guiding plan will not only offer management a clear focus, it will give the board a sound basis for oversight and for evaluating performance.

But above all, the staff—whether the executive, a development officer, or volunteers acting as staff—must take the initiative, constantly generating ideas that will move the fundraising forward and motivate board members' action.

How to motivate board members, especially those who have demonstrated a reluctance about fundraising, is a problem in itself. A strong board president or chair will get members to do their job. But the executive and staff can also stimulate trustee participation. They can engage trustees in simple projects, one project at a time, small tasks before large ones, making each task specific and limited. If trustees are asked individually to carry out a particular job, rather than appealed to generally in a board meeting, they will respond. Trustees are no different from others: they need to be *individually* stimulated, instructed, encouraged, and thanked profusely. And given the credit.

This motivating task of the executive and staff is not easy, but successful fundraising depends on its being fulfilled.

What Trustees Can Do

It is commonplace for board members to be reluctant, sometimes even resistant, to participate in fundraising. Many people associate fundraising with preying on friends or begging; others fear being turned down. Some will say their contribution to the organization is in the program, or administration, not in fundraising. Others will say they were not told that fundraising was part of being a board member.

Even if board members accept in principle their responsibility to participate, when it comes to action they frequently fall short in fulfilling commitments, and procrastination is ever-present. To overcome resistance, trustees need to understand some fundamentals:

- People give money because they want to. In raising money you do not need to twist arms or beg.

- People want to give money to worthy and successful endeavors that are making a difference. You must believe your organization does make that difference.

- People give money to people, not to ideas. The personal relationship underlies most contributions, especially major gifts.

Without acceptance of these truths, you won't raise money.

To overcome the reluctance, you can also show a trustee the many activities that assist the fundraising effort but don't actually ask for money. Many trustees, even those who most want to help, don't realize these opportunities exist.

Here in summary form you can see the many ways a trustee can materially assist the fundraising effort without actually asking for a contribution. (These fundraising actions are also presented in checklist form in Exhibit 11.1.)

- *Personal contribution.* All trustees, without exception, should make their own annual contribution to the organization. Regardless of the donations they may help to secure from other sources, this personal contribution is an essential act of commitment, no matter how small it has to be. No organization can expect others to invest in it if its leaders do not do so first. That investment starts with annual giving by board members.
- *Strategic planning.* Because institutional planning is so important to successful fundraising, a trustee must participate in determining the funding needs and in setting out the case for why people should contribute. (See Chapter Seven.)
- *Development plans.* As part of the board's oversight role and to assure participation in the development program, trustees should regularly approve the plans for raising funds prepared by the staff.
- *Adding to the mailing list.* The mailing list is at the core of the whole fundraising program. The names trustees add to that list are more valuable than those drawn from any other source.
- *Identifying and evaluating prospects.* Trustees are the peers of important prospective donors—individuals, officials of companies, and foundations. They know them, and their help in evaluation is invaluable.

Exhibit 11.1. Board Participation in Fundraising.
_____

For each item, score yourself and the board as a whole for level of participation; 1 (low) to 5 (high).

	self	board
1. Make personal contributions	____	____
2. Participate in strategic planning	____	____
3. Understand and endorse development plans	____	____
4. Add names to the mailing list	____	____
5. Help identify and evaluate prospects (individuals, foundations, corporations, religious institutions, service clubs)		
6. Share in cultivation of key prospects	____	____
7. Make introductions to prospects	____	____
8. Write notes on annual appeal letters	____	____
9. Participate in phonathons	____	____
10. Write supporting letters	____	____
11. Help manage fundraising events	____	____
12. Write thank-you letters	____	____
13. Accompany others in an asking	____	____
14. Ask for a contribution	____	____

Also ask yourself if you and others:

15. Actually do what you undertake to do	____	____
16. Manage to avoid procrastination	____	____
_____

- *Cultivating prospects.* A trustee who becomes identified with the organization can speak out in the community and can help interest prospective donors.
- *Introductions.* The most difficult part of a solicitation may be gaining the first introduction, especially to corporations and foundations. Trustees, because of their familiarity with the corporations and their standing in the community, can make the all-important introduction.
- *Annual appeal letters.* When trustees append personal notes to appeal letters, success will increase four- or fivefold. Appeals preceded or followed by phonathons give further opportunity for valuable trustee participation.

- *Supporting letters.* Organizations seeking support from a gov-ernment agency, foundation, or company, must submit a formal pro-posal. A separate supporting letter from a trustee does much to assure a favorable reading.

- *Special events.* Special benefit events are not only sources of money, they also help heighten the exposure of the organization; they are a form of public relations, of cultivation. Certainly board members will attend these events, but in addition it is particularly appropriate for board volunteers to manage them. This ensures that the event will not divert staff from their program responsibilities—a common problem.

- *Acknowledgments.* Letters of thanks for a donation are the first step toward the next asking. When a trustee adds an acknowledg-ing thanks, it is particularly effective.

- *Accompanying on an ask.* When a trustee accompanies the executive, a staff member, or another trustee in making a solicita-tion, it adds great weight. Moreover, it is the best way for a trustee to become familiar with the process of asking.

Raising Capital Funds

A whole new dimension of board participation comes into play when an organization turns to raising capital funds for buildings, endowment, or a reserve fund established to function as endow-ment, or when it seeks capital donations through *planned giving.*

Planned giving is a structured form of contributing assets. The recipient institution receives the donation only after an interven-ing period—often years—during which time the donor and a ben-eficiary may retain the use of the property or the lifetime right to receive its income. Such gifts, closely associated with estate plan-ning, can be in the form of bequests, insurance, real property, or securities.

Campaigns to raise capital funds, including planned giving pro-grams, demand the full commitment and participation of the board.

Capital donations, because they are large, usually involve board members directly in the identification, evaluation, cultivation, and solicitation of donors.

Oversight Responsibilities

The board's oversight responsibilities, described in Chapter Ten, extend to fundraising. In fact, watching over the fundraising effort puts special demands on the board. Two areas in particular warrant your attention: ethics and costs.

Through innocence or unrestrained aggressiveness, organizations can easily overstep the bounds of acceptable practice in seeking funding support. One clear ethical misstep to guard against is any fundraising carried out on a commission basis. Rewarding the fundraiser with a percentage of the money received, while not illegal, is considered professionally unethical—a fact not understood by many board members unfamiliar with unscrupulous fundraising agents.

It is also considered unethical to pay finder's fees to those who are in a position to help people with their estate planning for steering bequests or major gifts to an organization the donor may not have shown any interest in supporting. The donor's wish to make the contribution to a specific organization should be the dominant motivation.

In terms of managing costs, the expense of a fundraising program should not be excessive in relation to the amount raised. Determining reasonable fundraising costs, however, is by no means simple. Costs will vary widely with the size of the organization and the type of fundraising. For example, the costs of soliciting corporations, foundations, and individuals who are part of the organization's own constituency are unlikely to be worrisome. On the other hand, large national, high-profile organizations depend heavily on mass mail technique, which can be very expensive.

Be cautious about using mass mailing, often called direct mail.

The important distinction to make is between appeals to the organization's own mailing list—constituency mailing—and mass mailings to lists purchased, leased, or exchanged. The costs of constituency mailings tend to be modest; mass mail can be very expensive.

You may be exposed to other problems in the oversight of a fundraising program, such as public unhappiness with overly repetitious mail appeals, aggressive phone solicitations, and indiscriminate sales and exchanges of mailing lists. Several leading national philanthropic associations developed the Donor Bill of Rights (see Resource A) to serve as a reasonable guide.

To help them understand the fundraising program, particularly their oversight responsibility for the development program, boards, and especially development committees of boards, can ask the staff to prepare a comprehensive development plan, a strategy to be reviewed annually. A sample outline of a development plan is set out in Exhibit 11.2.

You will find fundraising to be one of the board's major preoccupations. To do your job well, you will need to understand its ramifications and participate wholeheartedly.

. . . .

What's the best solution when an organization is having trouble raising funds?

First, seek to understand the problem.

To begin with, make sure you're really talking about fundraising. Fees, contracts, tuitions, tickets, and reimbursements are *earned revenues*; fundraising is limited to *contributions*—donations and grants. Increasing revenues may be important, but don't confuse it with fundraising.

Remember that fundraising is a process. It is not a series of single ideas for raising money. Nor is it the same as mounting an expensive public relations campaign or putting on a fancy benefit. Rather it is continuous work by staff and board members, working

---

Exhibit 11.2. Outline of a Development Plan.

I. Core Elements

    A. Sources of Support (prepare a separate plan for each source)
        1. Individuals
            a. Annual giving or memberships
            b. Mass direct mail
            c. Major gifts
            d. Fundraising events
        2. Business
        3. Foundations
        4. Other nonprofit organizations
        5. Government grants
    B. Special Projects (prepare a separate plan for each project, such as:)
        1. Benefit events
        2. In-kind donations
        3. Fellowships
        4. Promotional projects and events
    C. Fundraising Process (prepare a separate plan for each administrative project, such as:)
        1. Preparing the case
        2. Strengthening the mailing list
        3. Strengthening the computer or filing system
        4. Strategic institutional planning
        5. Preparing the annual report or other printed materials

II. Components of Each Element (prepare for each element)

    A. Purpose: brief general statement
    B. Present Status: what is now being done
    C. Courses of Action: planned steps to be taken
    D. Targets: specific markers of achievement and schedule
    E. Administration: who is responsible; what is cost?

---

as partners, taking action in accordance with an agreed-upon plan with target goals to shoot for.

And don't forget that fundraising takes time. It is foolish to think you can suddenly raise $15,000, $50,000, or $100,000 to meet a cash-flow crunch. Whether you are seeking contributions from individuals, foundations, corporations, or government agencies, it can take months, if not years, before significant money comes in.

Then, after you have nailed down what your problem is, take these actions:

1. *Review your strategic plans.* The board, with staff support, undertakes comprehensive institutional planning (see Chapter Seven), setting out the vision of what the organization wants to be in the coming years, the programs that will fulfill that vision, the priorities among the programs, and the funding needs for those programs. What emerges is a comprehensive understanding of the mission for which you will be asking support. If you're meeting resistance, that may be a signal that your basic plan needs review and reevaluation.

2. *Make the case in writing.* The staff, in cooperation with the board, prepares the case, which is a persuasive statement of why people should support the organization. The case statement, which is not the same as the mission but is based on it, looks at the organization with the eyes of the donor. It is a prospectus for investment, a concept to be used throughout the fundraising effort, but particularly to attract the initial attention and interest of prospects. Often the case is best expressed in a brief memorandum, no more than two pages long.

The most persuasive case statements start with an identification of the need—what is missing, why the organization exists. Only after that does it describe what the organization does, how it does it, and who the organization is.

Most organizations have mission statements; few have an adequate statement of the case.

3. *Explore all your sources.* Staff and board together then make plans to solicit prospects in each category—government agencies, companies, foundations, other nonprofit organizations, and individuals—and establish priorities among them so that the effort is put where the prospects are best.

4. *Promote annual giving.* Those who make regular annual contributions, including those you call members, are the underlying strength of most nonprofit organizations. Pay a lot of attention to them. The mailing list is the backbone of successful annual giving; it should be diligently maintained and constantly increased.

5. *Hold fundraising events with caution.* Beware of diverting attention to, or relying on, benefits and fundraising events. Ideas for such events are a dime a dozen but the competition for attendance is staggering. Mounting events is labor intensive, and too often the work is put upon a busy staff. The first step for a special event is to find a volunteer who can and will run it. Without that person, forget it.

Do these things and you are on your way to successful fundraising.

• • • • • • •

Is it reasonable to set a level of financial contribution for all board members?

Clearly every board member should, as an act of commitment, make an annual personal contribution; everyone is capable of giving something, no matter how small. Many organizations, however, call upon every board member to give, or get others to give, a prescribed amount. This is sometimes described as a "give, get, or get off" policy.

The subject is controversial; strong views are held both for and against. The principal argument for is that if a specific amount is set for board members they will be stimulated into giving at a higher level than they otherwise would, and a larger total board contribution will be realized.

Arguments against are several. First, by setting a figure, you are in effect presenting a ceiling. People, board members included, are inclined to accept the suggested amount. Even if you ask that people give at least the set figure, you still risk missing higher gifts.

Also, this policy assumes a general equality in board members' capability to give and ability to attract contributions from others. Not only is there inevitably a wide disparity among members in both capability and ability, the policy runs at cross purposes to a board's need to achieve diversity in gender, age, race, occupation, skills, and constituency representation.

It is difficult to enforce. The inevitable exceptions and compromises can be troublesome and bring into question the board's consistency and the validity of the policy itself.

And finally, the basic esprit of the board is reduced when you put a monetary value on membership.

On balance, the nays would seem to have it. Boards will want to recruit some members who can make major financial contributions and attract others to contribute. But not all members should be expected to be in this category.

12

Keeping the Board Effective

An effective board is absolutely essential to an effective organization. Sound governance is as important as sound management. As a board member, therefore, you need to be sure the board keeps an eye on itself to determine it is doing its job well.

If you are a trustee of a public service organization (rather than one that exists to serve only its members), you must be constantly mindful of the comprehensive nature of your fiduciary responsibility. Nonprofit organizations are not democracies where interests and constituencies are represented in a parliamentary sense and decisions are made by votes or by people speaking on behalf of special interests. Rather, in public service organizations, board members are trustees of a public interest; they have a responsibility to make decisions in the interest of the organization as a whole, not as representatives of any sector. Although members are, and should be, drawn from different regions, backgrounds, and interests, it is wrong to think of the board as a representational body composed of delegates.

George Overton, Chicago lawyer and leader of the American Bar Association's studies of nonprofit organizations, explains that a board does not have "little islands of concern: Jones is here to raise money, Brown knows about personnel issues, Smith served on a similar board and knows the issues. . . . Those may be considerations for the nominating committee, but once on the board, all pull at the oars; there shall be no islands of authority" (1993).

There are two good ways for a board to go about assuring its own effectiveness. One is periodically to undertake a self-assessment. Such an exercise can be led by an outside, objective professional, but if not, any considered effort by the board to hold a mirror up to itself can be valuable.

A useful tool for a self-assessment is Exhibit 12.1, a checklist based on the seven basic responsibilities described in Chapter Five. Board members can review the list individually or working as a group.

In any such self-assessment, in addition to reviewing its performance in fulfilling responsibilities, a board should examine its organization and procedures. This is discussed in Chapter Thirteen, which also includes a separate checklist (Exhibit 13.1) covering these aspects of board effectiveness.

Another way for a board to keep tabs on its own effectiveness is to mandate a standing committee to do precisely that: constantly watch over the board's activities and its fulfillment of its responsibilities, and report regularly to the board on its review, with recommendations.

This committee (it may be called the committee on trustees or the governance committee) can also assume the responsibilities of a nominating committee, but its broader function is to keep all the operating procedures of the board under surveillance: its meetings, its paperwork, its committee activities, its board–staff relations, its planning procedures—anything that relates to board effectiveness or anything the chair asks it to look into. Clearly, oversight of conflict of interest, discussed in Chapter Fourteen, would fall within the purview of such a committee.

The chair of the governance committee needs to be one who commands the respect of the board members. A person with experience as board chair for another organization is usually an excellent choice.

When you consider the matter of board effectiveness, don't overlook the role of the executive in assisting the board. Some

Exhibit 12.1. What Is Expected of a Board Member.
_____

For each of the seven responsibilities, rate yourself and the board as a whole; from 1 (low) to 5 (high).

	self	board
1. *Attendance*		
To attend board meetings	___	___
To participate in some committee activity	___	___
2. *Mission*		
To determine the mission	___	___
To participate in planning, periodically reviewing the purposes, priorities, funding needs, and set targets of achievement	___	___
3. *Chief executive*		
To approve the selection and compensation of the chief executive	___	___
To assure regular evaluation of the performance of the chief executive	___	___
4. *Finances*		
To approve an annual budget and oversee adherence to it	___	___
To contract for an independent audit	___	___
To control investment policies and management of capital funds	___	___
5. *Program oversight and support*		
To support staff	___	___
To oversee and evaluate programs	___	___
To be an advocate in the community	___	___
6. *Fundraising*		
To contribute personally and annually	___	___
To participate in seeking funding resources	___	___
7. *Board effectiveness*		
To assure fulfillment of responsibilities	___	___
To maintain strong organization and procedures	___	___

people maintain that the most important single job of a chief executive is to help the board be effective.

Quite apart from being the organization's senior manager, the executive can guide the chair and help individual members and the board as a whole keep the board strong and functioning well. The executive, assisted by staff, can help the board establish and maintain a sound structure and organization, make meetings interesting and productive, and guide committee work.

While the executive can be helpful in the recruitment of new board members, be sure to guard against the executive who packs the board with personal supporters.

It is surprising how many nonprofit boards overlook the importance of assuring their own performance in the overall effectiveness of the organization. As a trustee you would do well to be alert to it.

· · · · · · ·

Can the domination of an organization by one person be a serious danger to it?

Yes.

A common manifestation of this malady is called "founderitis": a founding executive or early chair who can't or won't let go. The person may be strong and a good leader who still contributes significantly to the organization's effectiveness, but he or she so dominates decisions that the rest of the board is effectively disenfranchised.

It is sad and difficult when the leader cannot let go, cannot recognize that a board must be free to deal with new conditions that call for innovative decisions. A mark of leadership is the ability to deal effectively with change, and one change can be a call for new leadership. An orderly succession into a new phase of the organization's life may be impossible without change.

You as a single board member may feel that your hands are tied when you see these conditions in your organization. Continue to stress at every opportunity the corporate responsibility of the whole board for the life and performance of your organization. You will soon be heard—if rescue is indeed possible. Perhaps your function on the board is just that: tactfully, patiently, and constructively to bring about this major change.

Part III

Board Members and Boards

. . . .

13

Board Organization and Procedures

If a nonprofit board is to fulfill its responsibilities and function effectively as a group, it must deal with a number of organizational and procedural matters: its *composition*, *recruitment of members*, *officers*, *committee structure*, and *meetings*. These determinations flow directly from the original charter of the organization and are put into the bylaws to set the pattern of board operation. They can be changed by the board when it chooses to manage its affairs differently.

Board members will do well to be conscious of these organizational and procedural issues—the process—while they are fulfilling the seven responsibilities expected of them.

Although each organization has its own personality and chooses its own course and pattern of operation, there are some commonalities.

Composition

You will find rather quickly that the size and composition of the board can be a controversial subject. Nonprofit boards tend for several reasons to be fairly large. Numbers will assure that the views and needs of various constituencies are understood and properly served. Numbers will allow for diversity in age, race, and gender. Numbers in particular will permit a board to draw in members of three kinds that every board should have: those with knowledge and experience in the program area; those who have professional skills helpful in guiding the organization—legal, accounting, fundraising, public relations, and the like; and those with prestige in the community, people who have access to funding sources.

Accordingly, most nonprofit boards find it necessary to have at least twenty members. However, when membership runs to forty and more, interest is hard to sustain and decision making becomes increasingly difficult. Organizations wishing to retain the involvement of more strong supporters than its board membership can accommodate sometimes form councils or advisory committees. But even then, it is the trustee board that actually governs.

Recruitment of Members

The charters of some institutions call for trustees to be selected by an outside authority (as with regents in state universities) or elected by members of a broader organization (as with professional societies or trade unions). This discussion concerns nonprofit organizations whose boards are self-perpetuating; that is, where the board selects its own members for terms of its own choosing.

Boards can maintain vitality by limiting the terms of appointment. Members are elected to serve terms of two, three, or four years. Often two successive terms are permitted, but then the person must take a year off before being eligible to return to the board. Valued members can thus be reengaged while those not attending and participating can simply not be reelected. Staggered terms—not bringing up all members for reelection at the same time—achieve continuity.

Recruiting new members deserves continued high priority. Knauft and associates state, "The dynamic board . . . pays close attention to the character and diversity of its membership. It regularly seeks out new blood, not only as a source of new ideas, but to renew itself and adapt to changing circumstances in ways that help the organization achieve its mission" (Knauft, Berger, and Gray, 1991).

Judith Nelson, a Washington, D.C., consultant, adds, "[The] heart of your nonprofit should be composed of active leaders of diverse backgrounds who work individually, and as a team, on behalf of the organization. The process by which you identify board candidates and then cultivate, recruit, orient, involve, and acknowledge each new member will be central to the overall and long-term effectiveness of your nonprofit" (1991).

On the other hand, former Rockefeller Foundation president Lyman, noting that the board's role tends to be that of responding rather than of taking initiatives, points to a dilemma that bears directly on the recruitment of members: "In identifying the ablest and best candidates for governing board membership, the appointing authority naturally looks for individuals of extraordinary achievements, movers and shakers, people who have a reputation for success in making things happen. Yet, once appointed or elected to a board, the new trustee . . . for the most part is expected to join his or her colleagues in waiting to act until asked to do so by the administration" (1985).

Every board member should feel a keen responsibility to keep the board membership strong. Once having defined the needs, diligent board members can identify and help in the recruitment of new members.

Asking someone to join the board is itself a sensitive matter. You don't want to invite people to join unless you can be assured the board will elect them. On the other hand, you don't want to put a name up for election to the board unless you have reason to believe the election will be accepted. You may have to go through a minuet: first an informal testing of the board, then of the prospect.

The actual invitation for a prestigious person to join the board can be as important as soliciting a major gift and should be treated similarly. Choose carefully the right person to do the asking: rarely the executive or a staff member, often the chair, always someone the candidate respects. Ask in person, preferably by a visit rather than by phone or letter.

An important aspect of recruiting is to install a regular procedure for orientation of new members. It is not difficult to arrange but it is sometimes overlooked. In fact, periodic orientation of veteran trustees is highly valuable.

Because of the importance and the difficult ramifications of the recruitment process, many boards consider the chair of the nominating committee the most important of all committee positions.

Officers

Deciding what officers you need and establishing an election process do not usually present difficulty. But the importance of assuring strong leadership can't be overstated.

Turnover of leadership is healthy. One way to ensure it is with limited terms for officers, especially the chair or president of the board. Some organizations find it useful to keep the succession orderly by grooming the vice chair to take over; others find the system restrictive.

A nominating committee should be able to keep attention on the succession, get a sense of fellow member views, and make nominations.

Committee Structure

Overall board effectiveness depends in good part on useful committee work. As a board member it is worth your while to put attention on the organization of committees, but do make sure that the board does not, except in special circumstances, delegate to committees the board's responsibility.

The board should charge committees to keep subjects under review, focus the board on those things that need board attention, and make constructive recommendations for board decision. Exceptions where a board may in fact delegate its responsibility include capital investment management, managing a capital campaign, or running a fundraising event.

Boards can suffer either by too much or too little committee activity, either risking encroachment into management or causing the full board to get enmeshed in matters a committee could have sifted through.

Most boards have need for committees to concern themselves with at least the following matters: finance/budget, development/fundraising, and nominating (or governance committee). But others may also be appropriate: an audit committee, a personnel policy committee, an executive evaluation committee, a building or facilities committee, or committees particular to specialized activities of a school, museum, or theater.

Be on the alert for two kinds of committees that can be controversial. An executive committee can be useful, even essential, if its authority is confined to taking necessary actions between board meetings. But when an executive committee makes decisions in place of the board, or reviews and virtually decides matters before they come to the board, the responsibility—and the interest—of board members are significantly diminished. In a word, the stronger the executive committee, the weaker the board is likely to be.

Program committees—those set up to oversee the substantive programs of an organization—run the risk of dominating program management. Boards do have an undeniable oversight responsibility to evaluate the performance of the substantive programs; if that oversight cannot be effectively handled by a full board, a committee, or perhaps several committees, may be needed. In establishing those committees, however, the line between governance oversight and executive management must not be allowed to disturb board–executive cooperation.

Be precise in the charge to each committee. A helpful procedure is to call for each committee to set out annually its plans and targets for the coming year. This exercise helps the committee sharpen its purposes and also sets up a basis for evaluating its achievement.

Meetings

Board attendance and participation hinge on well-planned meetings. As a member you can hold the board chair and executive to their special charge to make the meetings interesting, with full opportunity for open discussion.

Many things combine to make meetings successful. Setting the times and place can be critical. So also can be the preparation of papers to be discussed—not too many, not too long and complicated. When people are not given adequate and timely preparatory materials, they are unable to participate knowledgeably; overwhelmed by paperwork, they become frustrated.

Board members want to keep in touch with program matters and not let board meetings get regularly bogged down with budgets, fundraising, and administration. Ignoring the programs the organization exists to provide can cause board member interest to wane.

As part of a self-assessment exercise (see Chapter Twelve), a board could find it helpful to use a checklist on organization and procedures, as outlined in Exhibit 13.1.

Exhibit 13.1. Board Organization and Procedures.

Rate your own board, from 1 (low) to 5 (high).

1. *Composition*
   a. Size _____
   b. Diversity _____
   c. Program knowledge _____
   d. Community knowledge _____
   e. Skills _____
   f. Prestige _____

2. *Recruitment of members*
   a. Tenure and rotation of members _____
   b. Identification of board needs _____
   c. Canvas of candidates _____
   d. Persuasive invitations _____
   e. Orientation _____
   f. Nominating committee's performance _____

3. *Officers*
   a. Positions and terms _____
   b. Selection _____
   c. Performance _____

4. *Committee structure*
   a. Number and roles _____
   b. Terms of reference _____
   c. Performance _____
   d. Executive committee _____

5. *Meetings*
   a. Frequency, time and place _____
   b. Agendas _____
   c. Papers _____
   d. Openness of discussion _____
   e. Interest _____

. . . .

Rights, Obligations, and Liabilities
of Board Members

Much is expected of you as a trustee, but you have a right to expect much in return from an organization. There are also legal obligations and some risks you have to consider as a trustee.

Rights

A trustee should be able to count on others—fellow board members, the executive staff—to act as partners working together to carry out the organization's mission. You should be able to rely on a willingness of board colleagues to fulfill the responsibilities and work expectations of trusteeship.

Although it is difficult to assure it, you are also entitled to expect strong leadership—a chair with a vision of what the organization can be and the capacity to motivate people toward the fulfillment of that vision. It is especially important that the chair cause the board experience to be productive, interesting, and rewarding.

Obligations

In legal environments, board member obligations are sometimes described this way:

"All trustees have the duty to care—to attend, participate in decisions, and be reasonably informed on matters that relate to the decision; and the duty of loyalty—to exercise their powers in the interest of the organization, rather than in their own or anyone else's interest."

The duty to care principally calls for your diligent attention to the responsibilities of trusteeship discussed in earlier chapters: participating, keeping informed, and exercising independent judgment on decisions that come before the board. The duty of loyalty simply means that you not have another loyalty or interest that puts into question your loyalty as a trustee; that is, that you avoid any conflict of interest.

Boards and individual board members at their peril overlook their legal obligation to avoid such conflicts of interest. Regulations on the subject should be incorporated in the bylaws, and procedures established to assure compliance by both board members and staff.

At a minimum, trustees and staff should be called on to disclose, preferably in writing and annually, if they, or any person to whom they are related or affiliated, now transact or are planning to transact business with the institution. For some people such full disclosure satisfies the conflict problem, especially if the board asks for disclosure, including the value to the recipient, each time a contract or assignment is entered into.

Other experts, however, believe a more stringent stand should be taken to avoid conflicts of interest. They would question whether any trustee who is a professional—lawyer, accountant, real estate or insurance agent, banker, stockbroker, consultant, or other—should ever perform professional service for the organization. And they believe this is true regardless of whether the trustee in question works at a regular or reduced fee, is compensated indirectly in something other than cash, or even works pro bono.

Regardless of the strictness of the conflict principles, a key aspect of the problem centers on the process of selecting the person to be retained for professional services. For example, in securing legal assistance, you want to retain someone who is expert in the particular problem at hand, not one who happens, as a board member, to come free or at low cost. In contracting for many types of service, competitive bidding can avoid any conflict of interest, as well as help to secure the best person at the best price to perform the assignment.

Be clear on the distinction here: it is altogether fitting for professionals who are board members to give expert advice to help set policy and make decisions; being retained to provide professional services is what is questionable, some would say with a strong presumption against.

It is often a tough call, but you should be sure the board is explicit on how it handles such questions of conflict of interest. Its importance is magnified by the need to avoid even the appearance of conflict, let alone actual conflict. Some organizations try to solve the difficulty simply with the stricture, "if you have to ask, you shouldn't do it."

Liabilities

You may be concerned, as are many trustees or prospective volunteers for trusteeship, about the liability risks boards or individual trustees are exposed to, and how they can be avoided, reduced, or protected against by insurance.

George Webster, general counsel to the American Association of Association Executives, speaking for association directors but presumably with comparable validity for trustees of nonprofit public service organizations, summarizes the risks in this way: "From a purely statistical standpoint, it could be argued that personal liability of directors of associations is not a significant problem. Of all the thousands of decisions made by association boards of directors, only a very few actually result in liability. On the other hand, you must measure the level of risk against the potential consequences if liability is imposed" (Webster and Webster, 1994). In the final analysis, Webster says, the possibility is not sufficient cause to discourage volunteer service as an association director.

The subject of liability is vast and technical. While there can be no substitute for the counsel of legal and insurance professionals, some basics can help you understand the dimensions of the problem. Here are selected excerpts from an article entitled "Board Members and Risk: A Primer on Protection from Liability" (Butler, 1992).

> *State Volunteer-Protection Laws.* Historically, charitable organizations were not liable for their wrongful conduct. Although the doctrine of charitable immunity did not protect board members per se, existence of the doctrine undoubtedly contributed to a legal custom that inhibited suits against charitable boards. Today, however, practices have changed. In response to recent concern about the liability of volunteers, each of the 50 states has passed volunteer-protection laws that grant immunity from liability for board members in some cases.

> *Indemnification.* An organization may choose to indemnify its board members in the event of legal action by using its own resources to pay for costs associated with some liability suits. This practice, essentially self-insurance, presumes that the organization has the necessary resources to make the payments, not necessarily a valid assumption in case of all organizations.

> *General and Other Liability Insurance.* Virtually all organizations carry general liability insurance, as well as one or more specialized policies covering auto, property, malpractice, fiduciary, and other areas. Some of these policies cover board members in certain circumstances.

Director's and Officers' [D&O] Liability Insurance.
D&O liability insurance is the type of policy most carefully tailored to cover suits involving board actions. It is
designed for the special purpose of protecting board
members by paying defense costs, settlements, and judgments in some suits that challenge decisions they have
made.

This last point on D&O insurance is what concerns trustees
most directly. The NCNB publication points to some trends:

- For some types of nonprofits, experts estimate
  that as many as 90 percent of all claims involve
  employment-related issues (including discrimina-
  tion, wrongful termination, and harassment).

- Few volunteer board members have been found personally liable in a suit.

- Claims are almost always settled out of court before
  trial.

- Defense costs tend to be high even if suits are without merit.

The question of liability coverage has no simple answer. Should
a trustee insist on D&O insurance coverage, and if so what kind
is preferred? Criteria for the need is neither set nor agreed upon.
There is no standard policy. Huntington Block, a leading insurer of
nonprofit organizations, says, "No single form of insurance is more
generally misunderstood than D&O" (personal communication,
1994).

Nancy Axelrod, president of the National Center for Nonprofit
Board, notes that "D&O insurance does not and should not protect
individual board members from malfeasance or misconduct. . . .

Insurance coverage is not a substitute for diligent trusteeship and responsible governance" (Butler, 1992).

In summary, as a trustee you need to examine not only what an organization expects of you but also what you can expect of the organization in rights, obligations, and liabilities. Although negative aspects of trusteeship should be acknowledged, they should not discourage you from accepting a membership on a board. The risks can be avoided or put under protection.

• • • • • • •

What can a trustee do to avoid the problems that some prominent non-profit organizations have experienced—misuse of contributed funds and woeful lack of governing board oversight responsibility?
Trustees, it is clear, have the responsibility of seeing to it that their nonprofit organization serves a worthy cause, that it is run well and honestly, and that it raises and spends money prudently.

Two independent watchdog agencies, the Council of Better Business Bureaus (CBBB) and the National Charities Information Bureau (NCIB), have established standards for public accountability, use of funds, informational materials, fundraising practices, and governance. They regularly review organizations and issue statements on their conformity or nonconformity to the standards. These standards are presented in the Resource section of this book: CBBB's Standards for Charitable Solicitation (Resource B) and NCIB's Standards in Philanthropy (Resource C). Together they give a good measure of what you need to watch for.

Although you cannot protect yourself against all vulnerabilities, you can have confidence in the public accountability of your board if you pay close attention to the following five specific matters, each of which has been discussed in earlier chapters.

1. *The mission.* Be sure the job needs doing. Through strategic planning and oversight activities, the board has the opportunity to frequently review the mission to assure the organization indeed

fulfills a social need, is not an unnecessary duplication of other agencies, and does not seek to grow simply for the sake of growth.

2. *Audits*. Be sure the audit is handled by the board and that the board makes full use of its auditors. Close cooperation with the auditors would have saved some organizations that ran into trouble; it can save your organization from difficulty.

3. *Conflicts of interest*. Be sensitive to the dangers of conflicts of interest. They can be the curse of nonprofit boards. Board members who are professionals can advise on policies related to their expertise, but if they receive any compensation from the organization, a conflict of interest may arise. Full disclosure is the first step; then, in each case careful and conservative judgment on the merits is called for.

4. *Evaluation of the executive*. Even with a long-time, respected executive, a regular and thorough evaluation will enhance the governance–management relationship and give the board assurances that the executive continues to perform well.

5. *Keeping the board effective*. Make sure the board looks after its own effectiveness as well as that of the rest of the organization. Periodic self-assessment is needed. A standing committee can be charged with watching how the board is performing, monitoring its activities, and assuring that it is fulfilling its fiduciary responsibility, and thus is fully accountable. By keeping tabs on board procedures the committee can be a safeguard against complacency.

Nonprofit boards find themselves in deep difficulty when they fail to take the trouble to stay on top of these matters. Scandals that have arisen involving inappropriate, unethical, or illegal activities in nonprofit organizations could have been avoided had their boards been diligent in handling problems of this kind. Public accountability and fiduciary responsibility mean staying on guard.

Leadership:
Every Board Member Has a Role

L eadership, that elusive but ever-so-important quality, is what empowers an organization, gives it purpose and strength. Leadership consists of perceiving the direction to take, explaining it in a way that arouses the desire to follow, and then with commitment taking that path so others will follow.

In nonprofit organizations the qualities and characteristics that make for strong leadership should be found especially in the chairperson of the board, but also in the chief executive, even while managing the organization, and in the board as a whole.

John Gardner, who has written much on the subject of leadership, says that "leadership is not one thing; it's a variety of things" (1985). He points to these key aspects of leadership:

- *Affirming values.* the capacity to assert a vision of what the organization can be at its best.

- *Agenda setting.* identifying goals, sifting priorities, conceptualizing a course of action.

- *Motivating.* "leaders don't invent motivation, they unlock what is there."

- *Institution building.* "shared purposes of a group . . . are accomplished through institutions, and leaders who are

institution-builders tend to leave a more enduring
mark than those who are not."

- *Clarifying and defining.* finding the words and teaching,
leaders "help us understand what we are going
through."

- *Coalition building.* achieving "a workable level of unity,"
with a capacity to mediate, to resolve conflicts, to win
the trusts of all factions.

- *Renewing.* "every vital system reaffirms itself . . . to stay
vital to change and grow."

While all these elements are important, the task of motivating
has special significance for nonprofit organizations, dependent as
they are on volunteers and public support.

For strong leadership, look first to the chair. "To achieve its full
potential," Cyril Houle—former professor and dean at the University of Chicago and author of the book *Governing Boards*—says, "a
board must have a strong chairman whose primary task is to create
and maintain a spirit of unity among diverse people on the board
and to ensure that it works appropriately with the executive staff
in exercising effectively and ethically. . . . It is the chairman's task
to lead and to restrain, to blend in proper proportion the more capable and vocal members with the less experienced and silent ones"
(1989).

Selecting the chair therefore holds great importance for any
nonprofit organization. A successful charitable organization will
almost always have a strong chair. The continuation of positive
leadership is further secured when the chair prepares his or her own
successor. Conversely, experienced trustees can think of excruciat-
ing situations that reflected a lack of leadership: the chair who
doesn't attend meetings, is at cross purposes with the executive, lets
board discussion get out of hand, is slow to recognize the need to

find a constructive outcome of a debate, has stayed too long in office, is secretive, has a personal agenda, fails to work toward an orderly succession, and on and on.

On the other hand, don't underestimate the importance of the executive in meeting Gardner's elements of leadership. A strong executive will direct the staff, will clarify and define the mission, and will be the leading spokesperson for the organization. The executive will inspire the board as well as the staff, and will motivate all in fulfilling the mission.

And every board member has a leadership role to play. The enthusiasm and participation of trustees contribute to the effectiveness of the whole organization and so together are a force of leadership. Individual trustees can help turn a prevailing mode from negative to positive, or the reverse.

You as a trustee assume a share in leadership by your conscientious participation and by helping to select other members who will contribute their time and talent to the success of your organization.

Resources

Resource A

A Donor Bill of Rights

Philanthropy is based on voluntary action for the common good. It is a tradition of giving and sharing that is primary to the quality of life. To assure that philanthropy merits the respect and trust of the general public, and that donors and prospective donors can have full confidence in the not-for-profit organizations and causes they are asked to support, we declare that all donors have these rights:

I. To be informed of the organization's mission, of the way the organization intends to use donated resources, and of its capacity to use donations effectively for their intended purposes.

II. To be informed of the identity of those serving on the organization's governing board, and to expect the board to exercise prudent judgment in its stewardship responsibilities.

III. To have access to the organization's most recent financial statements.

IV. To be assured their gifts will be used for the purposes for which they were given.

This Bill of Rights was developed by the American Association of Fund Raising Counsel, the Association for Healthcare Philanthropy, the Council for Advancement and Support of Education, and the National Society of Fund Raising Executives; and was endorsed by the Independent Sector, the National Catholic Development Conference, the National Committee on Planned Giving, the National Council for Resource Development, and the United Way of America.

V. To receive appropriate acknowledgment and recognition.

VI. To be assured that information about their donations is handled with respect and with confidentiality to the extent provided by law.

VII. To expect that all relationships with individuals representing organizations of interest to the donor will be professional in nature.

VIII. To be informed whether those seeking donations are volunteers, employees of the organization or hired solicitors.

IX. To have the opportunity for their names to be deleted from mailing lists that an organization may intend to share.

X. To feel free to ask questions when making a donation and to receive prompt, truthful and forthright answers.

Resource B

· ·

The Council of Better Business Bureaus' Standards for Charitable Solicitations

Introduction

The Council of Better Business Bureaus promulgates these standards to promote ethical practices by philanthropic organizations. The Council of Better Business Bureaus believes that adherence to these standards by soliciting organizations will inspire public confidence, further the growth of public participation in philanthropy, and advance the objectives of responsible private initiative and self-regulation.

Both the public and soliciting organizations will benefit from voluntary disclosure of an organization's activities, finances, fund raising practices, and governance—information that donors and prospective donors will reasonably wish to consider.

These standards apply to publicly soliciting organizations that are tax exempt under section 501(c)(3) of the Internal Revenue Code, and to other organizations conducting charitable solicitations.

While the Council of Better Business Bureaus and its member Better Business Bureaus generally do not report on schools, colleges, or churches soliciting within their congregations, they encourage all soliciting organizations to adhere to these standards.

These standards were developed with professional and technical assistance from representatives of soliciting organizations, professional fund raising firms and associations, the accounting profession, corporate contributions officers, regulatory agencies, and the Better Business Bureau system. The Council of Better Business Bureaus is solely responsible for the contents of these standards.

For the Purposes of These Standards:

1. "Charitable solicitation" (or "solicitation") is any direct or indirect request for money, property, credit, volunteer service or other thing of value, to be given now or on a deferred basis, on the representation that it will be used for charitable, educational, religious, benevolent, patriotic, civic, or other philanthropic purposes. Solicitations include invitations to voting membership and appeals to voting members when a contribution is a principal requirement for membership.

2. "Soliciting organization" (or "organization") is any corporation, trust, group, partnership or individual engaged in a charitable solicitation; a "solicitor" is anyone engaged in a charitable solicitation.

3. The "public" includes individuals, groups, associations, corporations, foundations, institutions, and/or government agencies.

4. "Fund raising" includes a charitable solicitation; the activities, representations and materials which are an integral part of the planning, creation, production and communication of the solicitation; and the collection of the money, property, or other thing of value requested. Fund raising includes but is not limited to donor acquisition and renewal, development, fund or resource development, member or membership development, and contract or grant procurement.

Public Accountability

1. Soliciting organizations shall provide on request an annual report. The annual report, an annually-updated written account, shall present the organization's purposes; descriptions of overall programs, activities and accomplishments; eligibility to receive deductible contributions; information about the governing body and structure; and information about financial activities and financial position.

2. *Soliciting organizations shall provide on request complete annual financial statements.* The financial statements shall present the overall financial activities and financial position of the organization, shall be prepared in accordance with generally accepted accounting principles and reporting practices, and shall include the auditor's or treasurer's report, notes, and any supplementary schedules. When total annual income exceeds $100,000, the financial statements shall be audited in accordance with generally accepted auditing standards.

3. *Soliciting organizations' financial statements shall present adequate information to serve as a basis for informed decisions.* Information needed as a basis for informed decisions generally includes but is not limited to: a) significant categories of contributions and other income; b) expenses reported in categories corresponding to the descriptions of major programs and activities contained in the annual report, solicitations, and other informational materials; c) a detailed schedule of expenses by natural classification (e.g., salaries, employee benefits, occupancy, postage, etc.), presenting the natural expenses incurred for each major program and supporting activity; d) accurate presentation of all fund raising and administrative costs; and e) when a significant activity combines fund raising and one or more other purposes (e.g., door-to-door canvassing combining fund raising and social advocacy, or television broadcasts combining fund raising and religious ministry, or a direct mail campaign combining fund raising and public education), the financial statements shall specify the total cost of the multi-purpose activity and the basis for allocating its costs.

4. *Organizations receiving a substantial portion of their income through the fund raising activities of controlled or affiliated entities shall provide on request an accounting of all income received by and fund raising costs incurred by such entities.* Such entities include committees,

branches or chapters which are controlled by or affiliated with the benefiting organization, and for which a primary activity is raising funds to support the programs of the benefiting organization.

Use of Funds

1. A reasonable percentage of total income from all sources shall be applied to programs and activities directly related to the purposes for which the organization exists.

2. A reasonable percentage of public contributions shall be applied to the programs and activities described in solicitations, in accordance with donor expectations.

3. Fund raising costs shall be reasonable.

4. Total fund raising and administrative costs shall be reasonable. Reasonable use of funds requires that a) at least 50 percent of total income from all sources be spent on programs and activities directly related to the organization's purposes; b) at least 50 percent of public contributions be spent on the programs and activities described in solicitations, in accordance with donor expectations; c) fund raising costs not exceed 35 percent of related contributions; and d) total fund raising and administrative costs not exceed 50 percent of total income.

An organization which does not meet one or more of these percentage limitations may provide evidence to demonstrate that its use of funds is reasonable. The higher fund raising and administrative costs of a newly created organization, donor restrictions on the use of funds, exceptional bequests, a stigma associated with a cause, and environmental or political events beyond an organization's control are among the factors which may result in costs that are reasonable although they do not meet these percentage limitations.

5. Soliciting organizations shall substantiate on request their application of funds, in accordance with donor expectations, to the programs and activities described in solicitations.

6. Soliciting organizations shall establish and exercise adequate controls over disbursements.

Solicitations and Informational Materials

1. Solicitations and informational materials, distributed by any means, shall be accurate, truthful and not misleading, both in whole and in part.

2. Soliciting organizations shall substantiate on request that solicitations and informational materials, distributed by any means, are accurate, truthful and not misleading, in whole and in part.

3. Solicitations shall include a clear description of the programs and activities for which funds are requested. Solicitations which describe an issue, problem, need or event, but which do not clearly describe the programs or activities for which funds are requested will not meet this standard. Solicitations in which time or space restrictions apply shall identify a source from which written information is available.

4. Direct contact solicitations, including personal and telephone appeals, shall identify a) the solicitor and his/her relationship to the benefiting organization, b) the benefiting organization or cause and c) the programs and activities for which funds are requested.

5. Solicitations in conjunction with the sale of goods, services or admissions shall identify at the point of solicitation a) the benefiting organization, b) a source from which written information is available and c) the actual or anticipated portion of the sales or admission price to benefit the charitable organization or cause.

Fund Raising Practices

1. Soliciting organizations shall establish and exercise controls over fund raising activities conducted for their benefit by staff, volunteers, consultants, contractors, and controlled or affiliated entities, including commitment to writing of all fund raising contracts and agreements.

2. Soliciting organizations shall establish and exercise adequate controls over contributions.

3. Soliciting organizations shall honor donor requests for confidentiality and shall not publicize the identity of donors without prior written permission. Donor requests for confidentiality include but are not limited to requests that one's name not be used, exchanged, rented or sold.

4. *Fund raising shall be conducted without excessive pressure.* Excessive pressure in fund raising includes but is not limited to solicitations in the guise of invoices; harassment; intimidation or coercion, such as threats of public disclosure or economic retaliation; failure to inform recipients of unordered items that they are under no obligation to pay for or return them; and strongly emotional appeals which distort the organization's activities or beneficiaries.

Governance

1. *Soliciting organizations shall have an adequate governing structure.* Soliciting organizations shall have and operate in accordance with governing instruments (charter, articles of incorporation, bylaws, etc.) which set forth the organization's basic goals and purposes, and which define the organizational structure. The governing instruments shall define the body having final responsibility for and authority over the organization's policies and programs (including authority to amend the governing instruments), as well as any subordinate bodies to which specific responsibilities may be delegated.

An organization's governing structure shall be inadequate if any policy-making decisions of the governing body (board) or committee of board members having interim policy-making authority (executive committee) are made by fewer than three persons.

2. *Soliciting organizations shall have an active governing body.* An active governing body (board) exercises responsibility in establishing policies, retaining qualified executive leadership, and overseeing that leadership.

An active board meets formally at least three times annually, with meetings evenly spaced over the course of the year, and with a majority of the members in attendance (in person or by proxy) on average. Because the public reasonably expects board members to participate personally in policy decisions, the governing body is not active, and a roster of board members may be misleading, if a majority of the board members attend no formal board meetings in person over the course of a year.

If the full board meets only once annually, there shall be at least two additional, evenly spaced meetings during the year of an executive committee of board members having interim policy-making authority, with a majority of its members present in person, on average.

3. *Soliciting organizations shall have an independent governing body.* Organizations whose directly and/or indirectly compensated board members constitute more than one-fifth (20 percent) of the total voting membership of the board or of the executive committee will not meet this standard. (The ordained clergy of a publicly soliciting church, who serve as members of the church's policy-making governing body, are excepted from this 20 percent limitation, although they may be salaried by or receive support or sustenance from the church.) Organizations engaged in transactions in which board members have material conflicting interests resulting from any relationship or business affiliation will not meet this standard.

Resource C

· ·

National Charities Information Bureau's Standards in Philanthropy

National Charities Information Bureau (NCIB)

The National Charities Information Bureau was founded in 1918 by a group of national leaders who were concerned that Americans were giving millions of dollars to charitable organizations, particularly war relief organizations, that they knew little or nothing about.

Through the years, NCIB has evolved into an organization that promotes informed giving. NCIB believes that donors are entitled to accurate information about the charitable organizations that seek their support. NCIB also believes that well-informed givers should ask questions and make judgments that will lead to an improved level of performance by charitable organizations.

To help givers and charitable organizations, NCIB collects and analyzes information about charities and evaluates them according to the following standards.

Preamble

The support of philanthropic organizations soliciting funds from the general public is based on public trust. The most reliable evaluation

National Charities Information Bureau, Inc., 19 Union Square West, New York, NY 10003–3395, (212) 929–6300. The text of this resource was made possible by a grant from the Exxon Corporation.

of an organization is a detailed review. Yet the organization's compliance with the basic set of standards can indicate whether it is fulfilling its obligations to contributors, to those who benefit from its programs, and to the general public.

Responsibility for ensuring sound policy guidance and governance and for meeting these basic standards rests with the governing board, which is answerable to the public.

The National Charities Information Bureau recommends and applies the following nine standards as common measures of governance and management.

NCIB Standards

Governance, Policy and Program Fundamentals

NCIB *Interpretations and Applications*

1. Board Governance: The board is responsible for policy setting, fiscal guidance, and ongoing governance, and should regularly review the organization's policies, programs, and operations. The board should have

   Fiscal guidance includes responsibility for investment management decisions, for internal accounting controls, and for short- and long-term budgeting decisions.

   a. an independent, volunteer membership;

   The ability of individual board members to make independent decisions on behalf of the organization is critical. Existence of relationships that could interfere with this independence compromises the board.

   b. a minimum of 5 voting members;

   Many organizations need more than five members on the board. Five, however, is seen as the mini-

mum required for adequate governance.

c. an individual attendance policy;

Board membership should be more than honorary, and should involve active participation in board meetings.

d. specific terms of office for its officers and members;

e. in-person, face-to-face meetings, at least twice a year, evenly spaced, with a majority of voting members in attendance at each meeting;

Many board responsibilities may be carried out through committee actions, and such additional active board involvement should be encouraged. No level of committee involvement, however, can substitute for the face-to-face interaction of the full board in reviewing the organization's policy-making and program operations. As a rule, the full board should meet to discuss and ratify the organization's decisions and actions at least twice a year. If, however, the organization has an executive committee of at least five voting members, then three meetings of the executive committee, evenly spaced, with a majority in attendance, can substitute for one of the two full board meetings.

f. no fees to members for board service, but payments may be made for costs incurred as a result of board participation;

Organizations should recruit board members most qualified, regardless of their financial status, to join in making policy decisions. Costs related to a board member's participation could include such items as travel and daycare arrangements. Situations where board members derive financial benefits from board service should be avoided.

g. no more than one paid staff person member, usually the chief staff officer, who shall not chair the board or serve as treasurer;

h. policy guidelines to avoid material conflicts of interest involving board or staff;

In all instances where an organization's business or policy decisions can result in direct or indirect financial or personal benefit to a member of the board or staff, the decisions in question must be explicitly reviewed by the board with the members concerned absent.

i. no material conflicts of interest involving board or staff;

j. a policy promoting pluralism and diversity within the organization's board, staff, and constituencies.

Organizations vary widely in their ability to demonstrate pluralism and diversity. Every organization should establish a policy, consistent with its mission statement, that fosters such inclusiveness. An affirmative action program is an example of fulfilling this requirement.

2. Purpose: The organization's purpose, approved by the

The formal or abridged statement of purposes should appear board, should be formally and specifically stated.

3. Programs: The organization's activities should be consistent with its statement of purpose.

4. Information: Promotion, fund raising, and public information should describe accurately the organization's identity, purpose, programs, and financial needs.

with some frequency in organization publications and presentations.

Not every communication from an organization need contain all this descriptive information, but each one should include all accurate information relevant to its primary message.

There should be no material omissions, exaggerations of fact, misleading photographs, or any other practice which would tend to create a false impression or misunderstanding.

5. Financial Support and Related Activities: The board is accountable for all authorized activities generating financial support on the organization's behalf.

   a. fund-raising practices should encourage voluntary giving and should not apply unwarranted pressure;

   b. descriptive and financial information for all substantial income and for all revenue-generating activities conducted by the organization should be disclosed on request;

Such activities include, but are not limited to, fees for service, related and unrelated business ventures, and for-profit subsidiaries.

c. basic descriptive and financial information for income derived from authorized commercial activities, involving the organization's name, which are conducted by for-profit organizations, should be available. All public promotion of such commercial activity should either include this information or indicate that it is available from the organization.

Basic descriptive and financial information may vary depending on the promotional activity involved. Common elements would include, for example, the campaign time frame, the total amount or the percentage to be received by the organization, whether the organization's contributor list is made available to the for-profit company, and the campaign expenses directly incurred by the organization.

6. Use of Funds: The organization's use of funds should reflect consideration of current and future needs and resources in planning for program continuity. The organization should:

a. spend at least 60 percent of annual expenses for program activities;

b. insure that fund-raising expenses, in relation to fund-raising results, are reasonable over time;

Fund-raising methods available to organizations vary widely and often have very different costs. Overall, an organization's fund-raising expense should be reasonable in relation to the contributions received, which could include indirect contributions (such as federated campaign support), bequests (generally averaged over five years), and government grants.

c. have net assets available for the following fiscal year not usually more than twice the current year's expenses or the next year's budget, whichever is higher;

Reserve Funds

Unless specifically told otherwise, most contributors believe that their contributions are being applied to the current program needs identified by the organization.

Organizations may accumulate reserve funds in the interest of prudent management. Reserve funds in excess of the standard may be justified in special circumstances.

In all cases the needs of the constituency served should be the most important factor in determining and evaluating the appropriate level of available net assets.

d. not have a persistent and/ or increasing deficit in the unrestricted fund balance.

Deficits

An organization which incurs a deficit in its unrestricted fund balance should make every attempt to restore the fund balance as soon as possible. Any organization sustaining a substantial and persistent, or an increasing, deficit is at least in demonstrable financial danger, and may even be fiscally irresponsible. In its evaluations, NCIB will take into account evidence of remedial efforts.

Reporting and Fiscal Fundamentals

7. Annual Reporting: An annual report should be available on request, and should include

   Where an equivalent package of documentation, identified as such, is available and routinely supplied upon request, it may substitute for an annual report.

   a. an explicit narrative description of the organization's major activities, presented in the same major categories and covering the same fiscal period as the audited financial statements;

   b. a list of board members;

   The listing of board members should include some identifying information on each member.

   c. audited financial statements or, at a minimum, a comprehensive financial summary that (1) identifies all revenues in significant categories, (2) reports expenses in the same program, management/general, and fund-raising categories as in the audited financial statements, and (3) reports all ending balances. (When the annual report does not include the full audited financial statements, it should indicate that they are available on request.)

   In particular, financial summaries or extracts presented separately from the audited financial statements should be clearly related to the information in these statements and consistent with them.

8. Accountability: An organization should supply on request complete financial statements which

   a. are prepared in conformity with generally accepted accounting principles (GAAP), accompanied by a report of an independent certified public accountant, and reviewed by the board;

   To be able to make its financial analysis, NCIB may require more detailed information regarding the interpretation, applications and validation of GAAP guidelines used in the audit. Accountants can vary widely in their interpretations of GAAP guidelines, especially regarding such relatively new practices as multi-purpose allocations. NCIB may question some interpretations and applications.

   and

   b. fully disclose economic resources and obligations, including transactions with related parties and affiliated organizations, significant events affecting finances, and significant categories of income and expense;

   and should also supply

   c. a statement of functional allocation of expenses, in addition to such statements required by generally accepted accounting a principles to be included among the financial statements;

d. combined financial statements for a national organization operating with affiliates prepared in the foregoing manner.

9. Budget: The organization should prepare a detailed annual budget consistent with the major classifications in the audited financial statements, and approved by the board.

Program categories can change from year to year; the budget should still allow meaningful comparison with the previous year's financial statements, recast if necessary.

NCIB believes the spirit of these standards to be universally useful for all nonprofit organizations. However, for organizations less than three years old or with annual budgets of less than $100,000, greater flexibility in applying some of the standards may be appropriate.

References

Anthony, R. N. "The Financial Information That Nonprofit Trustees Need and How They Can Get It." *Nonprofit Management and Leadership*, Summer 1991.

Bowen, W. G. "When a Business Leader Joins a Nonprofit Board." *Harvard Business Review*, Sept./Oct. 1994.

Butler, J. (ed.). "Board Members and Risk: A Primer on Protection from Liability." *Board Member*, Oct./Nov. 1992 (special edition).

Carver, J. "Redefining the Board's Role in Fiscal Planning." *Nonprofit Management and Leadership*, Winter 1991.

Chait, R. P., Holland, T. P., and Taylor, B. E. *The Effective Board of Trustees*. Phoenix, Ariz.: Oryx Press, 1993.

Council of Better Business Bureaus. *Standards for Charitable Solicitations*. Arlington, Va.: Council of Better Business Bureaus, 1982.

Council of Better Business Bureaus. *Responsibilities of a Charity's Volunteer Board*. Arlington, Va.: Council of Better Business Bureaus, 1986.

Drucker, P. F. "Lessons for Successful Nonprofit Governance." *Nonprofit Management and Leadership*, Fall 1990.

Gardner, J. W. "Pursuing Leadership: All Levels, All Types." *AGB Reports*, Association of Governing Boards of Universities and Colleges, Jan./Feb. 1985.

Hodgkin, C. "Policy and Paper Clips: Rejecting the Lure of the Corporate Model." *Nonprofit Management and Leadership*, Summer 1993.

Holland, T. P., Leslie, D., and Holzhalb, C. "Culture and Change in Nonprofit Boards." *Nonprofit Management and Leadership*, Winter 1993.

Houle, C. O. *Governing Boards: Their Nature and Nurture*. San Francisco: Jossey-Bass, 1989.

Howe, F. *The Board Members' Guide to Fund Raising*. San Francisco: Jossey-Bass, 1994.

Independent Sector. *A Portrait of the Independent Sector*. Washington, D.C.: Independent Sector, 1993.

Knauft, E. B., Berger, R. A., and Gray, S. T. *Profiles of Excellence; Achieving Success in the Nonprofit Sector*. San Francisco: Jossey-Bass, 1991.

Lyman, R. W. "The Board's Job: Nurture Leadership." *AGB Reports*, Association of Governing Boards of Universities and Colleges, Jan./Feb. 1985.

Mathiasen, K. "Board Membering." Washington, D.C.: Management Assistance Group, 1986.

Merchant, K. E. Letters to the Editor. *Chronicle of Philanthropy*, Sept. 1990.

National Charities Information Bureau. "NCIB Standards." *Wise Giving Guide*, Dec. 1993.

Nelson, J. G. *A Guide to Building Your Board*. Washington, D.C.: National Center for Nonprofit Boards, 1991.

Overton, G. W. (ed.). *Guidebook for Directors of Nonprofit Corporations*. Chicago: American Bar Association, 1993.

"Wealth in America." *Town and Country*. 1994.

Webster, G. D., and Webster, H. K. "Avoiding Personal Liability." *Leadership*, American Society of Association Executives, 1994.

Index